HELP! They made me the

MANAGER

HOW TO LEAD SMART PEOPLE

TREVOR MANNING

Designed and Typeset by JOSEP Book Designs
josework@gmail.com

Paperback ISBN 978-0-6481915-8-2
eBook ISBN 978-0-6481915-9-9

CONTENTS

ENDORSEMENTS

This is a well written, easy to read book, for how to understand and utilize management skills. Unlike some books in this category, which are stuffy and textbook style, Trevor writes with engaging stories, where there are situations that are easily associated with the real world. I caught myself thinking that I was reading an interesting story, and at the end of the story I had new management skills. I highly recommend! **Dennis Adams, Global Technical Service Support, USA**

I was fortunate to benefit from Trevor's vast experience and coaching leadership during my first executive role which greatly assisted me as I navigated the associated challenges of the step up. The book really captures and articulates Trevor's true desire to help people succeed in a captivating manner. An exciting read based on situational circumstance rather than textbook theory. I highly recommend it. **Stuart Callender, Head of Technical Services, AUS**

I was very fortunate to have Trevor as my mentor for 10+ years as I made this leap from individual contributor to manager. The guidance in this book is invaluable to those taking that next step in their career into management. **Michael Crawford, Director of Operations, AUS**

This book really excels at sharing management concepts. **Stephen Dale, Assistant Vice President, Technical Services, USA**

Definitely Manning's magnum opus… an essential read covering all areas of management from remote working, communication, though to setting team objectives, skilfully wrapped in an engaging narrative. **Dave Edwards, Software Development Manager, UK**

This book was different to other management books I've read. It wasn't a textbook format. It was an easy read that I found SO relatable. I found myself laughing at the coffee shop scene - I felt like I was sitting there watching it! I highly recommend this book for anyone who leads a team in any industry. **Vanessa Edwards, National Podiatry Community & Disability Manager, AUS**

A really enjoyable read with such a unique approach to getting the message across. The wisdom displayed is a testament to your investment in your craft, and one that has undoubtedly helped in my career more than I can possibly explain. **Bryce Fisher, Wireless Technical Design Expert, UK**

I found this book to be very practical and easy to read. I enjoyed the analogies of the Grand Prix and the other stories, told in a unique way, through the two characters in the book: Chris and Sonya. I was able to relate both as a leader and as a coach. I would recommend this book for any emerging leader, new manager, and experienced managers. The advice is relevant and practical, especially for any technical resources moving into leadership roles. It left me feeling inspired. **Ocea Garriock, Coach and Leadership Enablement Facilitator, RSA**

As a technical professional with over 30 years' experience in the communications industry I found the techniques and examples helped me identify and then take stock of the wide range of skills I have developed throughout my career and to then re-apply this skill set to a management role. Even if you are early in your career the insights provided in this book will allow you to better understand what drives management decisions and how you can better support the common goals of your team to ultimately make your professional life far more fulfilling. A must-read for anyone making the transition from practitioner to manager role. **Aaron Gosschalk, Senior Delivery Technician, AUS**

Trevor has found a way of making all the complexities of management feel achievable in such an enjoyable and enthralling read! **Mitchell Hartas, Senior Rehabilitation Consultant, AUS**

This book engages the reader subconsciously in a way that ties together many aspects of leadership, with aha moments throughout the book. It will captivate any reader whose basic instincts are to lead and manage others. The book offers tactical, pragmatic approaches for dealing with real world situations, weaving a tapestry of tools and principles foundational to effective and rewarding leadership. The storyline is entertaining and engaging for first time and seasoned managers alike. Well worth the read. **Dennis Janda, VP Engineering, USA**

Unlike traditional management texts, this book combines real-world experiences with theoretical best-practise to bring to life both the challenges that new managers face, and the concepts they need in their 'toolbox' to be effective leaders. The story-telling throughout makes it an enjoyable read as well as an informative guide. **Sean Manning, Lead Solution Engineer, UK**

Everything in business and personal life is an evolution. There are no perfect rules or processes, so we learn with mixed results as we go. Trevor's book is a must read as it references and uses many well-known business publications "aha" grabs and links them into real life scenarios. These will put a lapsed manager back on track and in doing so compel them to pass it onto their aspiring managers and supervisors. For new managers this has got to be these best reference book going around. I wish I had this guidance when I was first promoted into management years ago. **Stuart McCullough, Group Sales Director, AUS**

This book is cleverly put together. I loved the winding through of research with an engaging story, and linking home and work examples, making it a pleasure to read. **Julie Mitchell, Leadership Consultant, AUS**

I wish I had this book when I inherited my first team and had to manage people who were previously my peers. The approach of providing theory and philosophy and then immediately explaining how to apply it, makes it a great format for a technical audience. **Alan Murphy, Director of Systems Engineering, USA**

What a wonderful read. This book demonstrates a perfect balance between theoretical concepts and pragmatic realism. It absolutely appeals to my learning style! I have already started applying these methods to my own leadership role. **Eddie Stephanou, Regional Technical Manager, AUS**

Management and leadership are more about experience than reading theories. This book blends the two to enhance the reader's knowledge as well as providing them practical ways to apply the concepts. **Kiera Young, Senior VP Customers, Products & Services, CA**

This book is so essential in the new world of remote working. It is critical that the roles and responsibilities are clearly identified and that knowledge workers understand the big picture and their role in achieving the big picture! This book provides a roadmap for the new manager to identify the requirements of his workforce and to lead them to a successful conclusion of the venture! I have yet to work with knowledge workers who would be enthusiastic in their work if they did not take ownership of the big picture and understand their role and contribution to the expected outcome. I am part of the development of the world's largest radio telescope with contributions from many hundreds of scientists and engineers from around the world - if the roles and boundaries are not clear to all parties very little would work on the first attempt costing the project a tremendous amount of money for rework! **Bruce Wallace, Senior Technical Consultant, RSA**

ACKNOWLEDGEMENTS

In my book, I point out that an F1 racing driver is the star of the show but winning is a team effort. I think being an author is similar. There are so many people involved to make a book a success.

First, I want to thank my wife Berry, who has worked tirelessly for many months handling all the editing and production of the book. Using the skills from my other book, "Help! I need to master critical conversations" she has given me brutally honest feedback in a skilful and kind way, resulting in a far better final product.

My beta readers also were fantastic in providing feedback that has enhanced the final text. I'd like to make special mention of a few people. Despite having a very senior role as Vice President of her company, Kiera Young provided detailed feedback and observations that shaped my thinking in the book's rewrite from that first beta version. Kate Jackson voiced a concern that the cover of the beta book did not do justice to the professionalism of the text inside, and it turned out many other people were thinking this but had not been brave enough to say anything. Alan Murphy wanted to know more about the team members, and so I developed a story around each team member in the revised book. Dave Edwards has an uncanny way of providing big picture feedback, noticing a continuity error in time or place and simultaneously noticing a double space error in the text. Dennis Janda, Neil Barnett, Stephen Dale, Susan Ottman, Dr Maragret Phillips, all busy people, took the time to provide me with pages of comments and observations. Thanks also to Vanessa Edwards and Mitch Hartas, who provided feedback from the perspective of the medical field.

I had over 100 people who kindly offered to be advanced readers, who did the final proofread. Some of their review comments are included in the Endorsement section.

Many people have told me how much they love the title, so I would like to thank those people who took part in the book title survey.

All the stories and experiences are true, so thanks to the many people I have had the pleasure of working and learning with, who make up the content of this book that hopefully will help others in their leadership journey.

I wrote this book to help others, and my thanks go to my virtual team of people mentioned above who helped make my ideas and insights the book you hold in hand today.

INTRODUCTION

Congratulations! You have been promoted to lead the team.

Chris stared at the promotion email he had just received. As exciting as this promotion was, he realised that it opened up a whole new world, and it had arrived with no practical training in day-to-day management. On the other hand, he had excelled in his MBA and was already the senior go-to person in the team. Even his previous manager often looked to him for help before surprising everyone with her sudden resignation.

'Where do I start?' Should I have a hands-off approach and trust and empower the team?'

Chris paused, 'Or should I become known as the manager that gets involved in understanding the details and helping the team?' Chris cupped his head in his hands. 'Oh, I don't know. If I help more and get stuck into the details, the team will accuse me of interfering and being a micro-manager. After all, some of my team members have been here longer than I have. If I don't get involved, they will accuse me of having my head in the clouds with no idea of what is going on.'

Chris is not alone. Managing skilled staff is not easy. Doctors, lawyers, teachers, accountants and even a barista hired at a local cafe develop advanced expertise and specialist skills in their trade. These skills are often beyond the scope of the people managing them. Even when the manager has expert technical skills themselves, they may find keeping up with the technological changes in our fast-paced modern world challenging. Yet, it is the manager who is held to account for everything that the team does.

Managing and leading skilled people effectively requires an understanding of the frame of reference of the team members. As a qualified engineer, Chris had spent a lifetime developing advanced skills that allowed him to design, build and fix things. He often thought that if he won the jackpot and retired early, he would continue to do engineering work. He loved designing a complex system, fixing something, writing new code for a software application, or just finding out how something works.

Chris was confident that at least he, as a technical person, understood how technical people think. His question was whether to empower his team and stay out of the way or to get actively involved in their activities.

While Chris was still musing over the email, the phone rang. It was his boss.

'Hey, Chris, congratulations. Your promotion has been formalised, and an all-company announcement will go out tomorrow. The management team is excited about your new role. We believe you will be great.

'To help you settle into your role, we have provided you with a dedicated business coach. We want you to work with her for the first 90 days, and after that, you can elect whether you want to continue the relationship. Her name is Sonya, and she will contact you. Good luck and, once again, well done. You deserve it.'

Sonya Miller reviewed her briefing notes for her latest assignment. Christopher Brown, a brilliant engineer, was newly appointed as the manager following *his* manager's resignation. Sonya made a mental note to dig deeper into why the previous manager had resigned. Chris's management had no concerns about his technical abilities. Sonya's assignment was to help to accelerate the development of Chris's management and leadership skills. Considering he was already the senior technical lead in the team, his bosses' concern was that he may be unaware of what was required to lead a team formally. Chris had developed no systematic methods for managing his work or the people around him and so would rely on working long hours to achieve his outputs. While this approach had worked well for him so far, his management feared that this would not be sustainable when managing a team of people. They wanted their staff to balance work life and home life, and Chris's habits of working late, even on weekends, worried them.

Sonya called Chris and arranged to meet him in his office the following day.

The phone call went well, but Sonya noticed how quickly he launched straight into the immediate issue on his mind. He made no attempt to build a relationship with her and spent no time explaining the bigger context of his situation.

Chris eventually stopped his soliloquy.

'So, Sonya, what is the right answer? Should I be a hands-on manager, or should I empower my team?'

'I tell you what. Let's meet up tomorrow morning in the office, and we can go over everything face to face.'

Chris's behaviour confirmed to Sonya that her choice of an *advice-driven* strategy for the coaching sessions was the right approach. In Sonya's earlier days of being a business coach, she had an over-simplistic view that her role was to only ask questions and to not provide any advice. When coaching experienced CEOs, a *question-only* coaching style stood her in good stead because there is nothing an experienced person likes less when seeking help than getting advice when they want a sounding board. Sonya realised that Chris was at the opposite end of the spectrum. He had not yet developed any basic competence in his role and needed advice and directive training rather than supportive coaching.

THE QUANTUM LEAP
INTO MANAGEMENT

Sonya sat down with Chris at his office. After exchanging the usual pleasantries, they got down to business.

'Chris, yesterday you asked me if you should be a hands-on manager or whether you should empower your team. There is no binary answer to that question. In management, you will need to learn to deal with contradiction and paradox. Running a team requires a balance of two opposite things: Autonomy and control.

'Autonomy is a major factor in motivation. Skilled people want to feel empowered and hate being told *what* to do. Skilled people also resent being told *how* and *when* to do something. The complication is that management structures and reporting lines mean that the person in charge, not the skilled worker, is held to account by *their* bosses for the results of the team.

'You cannot grant your team the autonomy they want without building and enforcing practical management disciplines and structures to ensure compliance with the minimum standards. That is where control comes in. You cannot have blind faith in your team and hope it all works out.'

'What? Are you saying I shouldn't trust my team?' Chris asked with wide eyes.

'We will talk about trust later,' Sonya promised and continued her point about the contradictions of autonomy *and* control.

'You need to understand the practical realities of both *managing* and *leading* a team in the real world. *Management* is about ensuring known activities are done in a structured and efficient manner. *Leadership* is about *changing* the status quo to a future desired outcome, through motivating yourself and others without initially knowing the details of how to get there.

'Chris, you will find that there is a massive transition in moving to this new management role. From what I have heard, you displayed leadership in your previous role, which is probably why you got promoted. Your challenge is now to add the management element without upsetting the balance between management and leadership.'

Chris was not the first skilled person to be targeted for management. Ironically, many skilled people are targeted due to their technical skills and yet get promoted into a management role, where a very different set of skills and a very unique way of thinking is required. Engineers end up being promoted to engineering managers, and accountants end up becoming CFO's, doctors end up running a hospital.

'Leading and managing smart people is not an easy task,' Sonya said. 'There is no magic wand, and I do not have all the answers. What I can help you with is providing frameworks and models, which will allow you to figure out the answers for yourself. Reading as much as you can from a variety of sources will also help you develop knowledge from different perspectives, and you can combine other people's experiences and insights with your own to develop your leadership abilities. And remember, you are managing and leading a team of living, breathing human beings. They are not machines.'

'Good point, Sonya, so where do I start?'

'Start by spending time with your team members and build a relationship.'

Sonya had brought along her favourite leadership book on how to manage a team. She reached into her bag and pulled out the book called *The Leader's Guide to Managing Teams.* 'This little textbook will provide you with the theory and practical guidance for managing a team. It will also give us a common language for our coaching sessions. Read chapter 1 before our session next week.'

Sonya left, and Chris's curiosity prompted him to open the book and start reading straight away.

THE QUANTUM LEAP INTO MANAGEMENT

In physics, a quantum leap refers to the sudden jump of an electron from one energy level to another. Quantum physics almost *defles* the law of physics by instantaneously jumping from one state to another. There is no gradual ramping-up process.

Management transition is the same. Technical people reach the point of being ready for promotion into management through years of education and developing advanced skills. Once promoted, they are immediately judged by a completely different set of criteria. Their technical skills become taken for granted. Expectations change, they change radically, and they change overnight:

What changes?

- Expectations from **management** change. Managers no longer judge the team leader based on their individual contribution or technical skill. Senior management expectations become about the technical manager's ability to manage and motivate the team.
- Expectations from **team members** change. Team members no longer judge the technical manager on their superior technical ability or experience. They judge them on their ability to help them and their ability to create a motivating environment.

- Lastly, expectations of **themselves** change. New managers vacillate between the often-conflicting needs of their *worker-self* and their *manager-self*. The *worker-self* feels frustrated about the way things are and expects the *manager-self* to fix it. New managers become at war with themselves.

A person's mindset about the role of a boss defines the way they behave as a manager. New managers may feel that everybody is looking to them as the expert who knows what to do, what decisions to make, and have the answers to *all* questions. As the realisation sinks in that they don't have the answers, they may feel wholly ill-equipped for this new role. After a few months of trying harder and putting in longer and longer hours, it is easy for a new manager to jump into an abyss of despair and frustration rather than make the quantum leap to a rewarding and satisfying management career.

The transition from a *technical expert* to a *manager* role requires a change in mindset. There is a saying, "If you always do what you have always done, then you will always get what you have always got."

Einstein said, "Doing the same thing over and over again and expecting different results is the definition of insanity."

Unfortunately, some managers don't always change their approach. They know it isn't working, but they don't know what the alternative is, and so they keep doing the same things.

Other managers abdicate their authority and, having lost complete control of the situation, just hope it all works out. Fortunately, there is a better way.

Chris shut the book decisively. He was not a fan of reading management books. They seemed wishy-washy compared to the data-heavy, analytical engineering textbooks that had helped him build his theoretical expertise. But he wanted to be successful in his role and so kept an open mind. He was also pleased that Sonya had offered practical advice telling him to start by building relationships with his team members. Chris returned to the office.

'Gather round everybody.' Chris said, pausing till everybody in the team formed an informal circle around him. 'As you saw in the company announcement, I have been appointed as the manager of the team. I am very excited to be given this opportunity and am looking forward to continuing to develop us into a high-performance team.'

Chris went on to share a high-level overview of what *management* was expecting of him and the team. Recalling Sonya's explanation of needing to both manage *and* lead, he also talked about basic things that he needed from the team and then told them he wanted to understand what they needed from him.

'I'd like to catch up with each of you in one-on-one meetings to hear your views.'

When Chris met with his team, he listened to their life and work stories to understand their perspective on the big picture. He realised that, despite working with some of them for years, he had never really gotten to know them. He avoided getting drawn into any specific operational issues, explaining that he would address them at a later date.

Chris found it easier talking to the younger and less experienced team members, as he felt they respected his experience and expertise. Two members of his team, Fred and Madison, were more experienced and older than he was. He felt an underlying scepticism on what value he could add to their roles and the unvoiced questions of why he got the manager role.

Most team members were not aware that the previous manager had been fired, and Chris did not feel it was his place to say anything. He hoped that with time, he would win over everyone in his team to respect his new management role.

Chris still had one team member he hadn't spoken to. Pierre Leroux, based in Paris at their French sister company.

Chris and Pierre had clashed on conference calls several times in the past, and Chris decided to let Pierre find out the news via the company announcement. He was not in the mood for a difficult conversation, and Pierre's negativity drained him.

Chris made a note to call him later in the week, then got stuck into his new role. He wanted to make a good impression and so worked enthusiastically on documenting a whole raft of ideas he had. Before Chris knew it, it was home time, but he realised he still had urgent issues to deal with that could not wait for the next day. He called home and explained that he would be late for dinner.

When he got home, he received a frosty greeting from his wife Gwen, who had prepared a celebratory dinner for his promotion. The atmosphere was tense, and he tried to make the best of the situation by offering ice cream to the kids after the meal. Gwen was unimpressed. The evening did not end well, and Chris had mixed emotions about the good news email that had kicked off his day.

The following week, Sonya popped her head around the screen that provided Chris with a modicum of privacy in his open-plan office. 'Fancy a cup of coffee? We can continue our discussion from last week on leadership.'

Sonya noticed the textbook sitting open on Chris's desk. 'Bring the book with you.'

When they arrived at the cafe located opposite the office, Sonya ordered a soy latte, and Chris ordered his usual morning wake-me-upper double shot cappuccino, extra hot. Sonya turned to face Chris.

'How did your first couple of days go being the new boss?'

'Well, someone needs to tell my family at home that I'm now in charge because nobody listens to me there. On my first day as manager, I left the office late, as I had to finish a few urgent things that couldn't wait for the next day. I didn't realise that my wife, Gwen, had prepared a celebratory dinner for my promotion, and I tried to make up for it by giving the kids their favourite ice cream. Afterwards, the kids played up from the sugar rush, and I ended up punishing them by confiscating their game consoles for 24 hours, resulting in a dispute between us adults on when and how to discipline the children. The evening did not end on a high note. So, why don't we change the subject and talk about my new role? How do I make sure that my team at work at least sees me as being in charge, even if I am not in charge at home?'

Sonya wanted to learn a bit more about his family, seeing as he had brought them into the conversation.

'How many kids do you have?'

'We have three kids. Evelyn is the oldest. She has just turned 13. Liam is 10. Our youngest is Nathan, who is 8.'

Chris didn't elaborate further, so Sonya took her cue from Chris that he didn't want to go any deeper into family matters and moved quickly back to discussing work.

'That's great, Chris. I am sure they are all very proud of you. The first fundamental principle to understand about leadership, at home or work, is that you are not *in charge.* At work, you own the outcomes of your team, but your team members are the leaders of the area they are working in. For example, Google interviews all software engineers for leadership skills, even if there is no expectation that any staff will ever report to them.'

Chris looked unconvinced. 'But surely it is important to hire software developers who are good at writing software? Why on earth would you choose someone with poor software skills just because they are good with people?'

Sonya took another sip of her latte. 'I did not say you would hire someone with poor software skills but having *good* software skills is a ticket-to-play. The *real differentiator* is showing leadership skills.'

Chris looked confused. 'But I thought that was *my* role? What is the point of having a team leader if the team members also do the team-leading?'

'Good question. Let's say a software developer knows that implementing specific user requirements from a customer *verbatim* will create unintentional consequences that the customer is unaware of. It requires leadership to operate outside their core role to get this resolved. It has nothing to do with managing the team, and it is not leadership in the traditional sense of the word. In this context, we are talking about proactive activities that, in the past, managers did that the staff now need to do.

'I mentioned that you would have to get good at contradiction and paradox in management. Showing initiative is important, but it is also important to know where showing initiative is no longer required nor desired. These boundaries are essential if the full empowerment of skilled staff is to operate effectively. This is one of the first models I want you to understand. It looks incredibly simple, and yet, once you understand it and know how to apply it, it will change everything in the way you go about your day. In fact, it can change the way you think about life and is the key to living a *happy* life, but we are getting ahead of ourselves.'

Sonya opened the *Leader's Guide* textbook she had given Chris earlier and said, 'read through this section before our coaching session later this week, and we can discuss the model further.'

3

LEADERSHIP BOUNDARIES

Chris looked dubious that the simple model he was looking at would change the way he thought about this moment, let alone his life, but regardless, he agreed to study the diagram.

Sonya left, and Chris thought he may as well read this section over a second cup of coffee.

LIMITS OF INFLUENCE

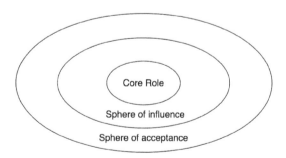

The job description, key performance indicators, formalised processes and a functional reporting structure define the **core role**.

Traditional management practices such as planning, organising, and control are relevant in the core. Typically, this is where functional measures are defined, which sets a minimum compliance line of acceptable performance. In the core, it is possible to determine *what* needs to be done and *how* to achieve it.

In the **sphere of influence,** people *elect* to get involved. They exhibit proactivity and initiative to improve and change the situation. There is no predefined course of action, and involvement is voluntary.

The outer zone is the **sphere of acceptance,** where exerting influence is unlikely to achieve anything. Knowing where this limit is, is essential to avoid unnecessary stress and frustration. No matter how senior someone is, there is always a limit to their actual power, authority, or influence.

On Thursday morning, Chris met up with Sonya in the office for his coaching session and opened the textbook to the Influence diagram.

'I think I understand everything that is written there, but I sense there may be a deeper meaning that I am not yet getting. You said this is the key to happiness. How does this diagram have anything to do with happiness?'

'Chris, the model helps you to categorise all the things you *have-to-do, elect-to-do,* and choose *not-to-do* in the appropriate spheres. The inner sphere represents the things in your core role at work or home. Usually, these consist of things you must do to be a competent worker or member of society. These things involve external expectations. We do them to comply with the norms of work and societal expectations. When we do them, they do not necessarily bring us happiness but provide us with a sense of fulfilling our duty.

'It is the middle sphere, where we find a deep sense of fulfilment because we elect to do things voluntarily. They appeal to our sense of wanting to find purpose and meaning. When we do these things, we feel we are making a real difference.

'The trick is to know where the limits of our voluntary activities lie. It is essential for people to only participate in the voluntary sphere when their core duties are done. It is unfair to others in the team if someone abandons their core role to go above-and-beyond and volunteer in a more interesting activity while leaving the rest of the team to fill the hole.

'At the opposite boundary of the voluntary sphere, trying to make a difference in areas where we have no influence leads to frustration, which arguably is the opposite of happiness. When you feel frustrated or use the word "should" a lot - "*but they should have told me*" - invariably you are no longer displaying effective leadership but operating in the outer sphere.'

'I can think of lots of examples that frustrate me.' Chris said. 'I want the world to be what it isn't. The bigger the gap between current reality and my goal, the more frustrated I feel.'

Chris paused to reflect. 'But didn't you say that leadership was exactly about that gap? You said leadership was about *changing* our current reality into our desired *future* outcome.'

'Remember, management involves contradiction and paradox, Chris. Effective leadership involves taking on challenges. Effective leadership also involves deliberately *not* taking on other challenges. Leadership is most effective when applied in the middle sphere - the sphere of influence.

'If you want to be happy at work, make sure you have your core role covered, then volunteer to help with things where you really can make a difference. For the rest, let it go. If you want to be happy in life, follow the same philosophy.'

Sonya opened her day planner. 'I will catch up with you again next Thursday. I am going away overseas for a few days the following week, so you will have plenty of time to read the rest of the chapter. You probably have heard of Frederick Winslow Taylor in your MBA management training. Read the book he wrote called *The Principles of Scientific management*. His ideas were strongly influential in the success of the Industrial Revolution, and it is worth studying what he really wrote, as opposed to misrepresentations of his ideas following his death. I am excited to be going to an international trade show in Paris that showcases his work.'

'One of my team members is based in Paris,' Chris said. 'To be honest,

I think I am going to struggle with managing him. He always seems negative and is disconnected from our team. Maybe you can meet up with him?'

'I'd love to do that. Send me his contact details.'

Sonya stood up to leave. 'In our next session, I'd like you to explain to me what you have learnt about the difference between leadership and management.'

ARE LEADERSHIP AND MANAGEMENT THE SAME THING?

It was Thursday afternoon, and Chris sat poised, ready to share his understanding of leadership and management with Sonya. He took a deep breath. 'Here goes.

'Management is about things and processes, and leadership is about people. For most situations in the management field, it is not an either-or choice but a balance between two opposite things. Instead of asking myself, "should I do A or B?" I am learning that I should ask myself, "what is the balance between A and B for the particular situation I am dealing with?"

'I am also learning that I need to focus on *management* more than *leadership* within my *core role,* where I know the predetermined outputs. The core sphere has predefined structure, process, and authority limits to *manage* risk. Management is about planning, organising, and controlling activities to achieve a predetermined output. Even for innovative and creative outputs, where we cannot know the details of the solution in advance, management is still essential for success.

'Management looks at the process of how we will organise ourselves and what structure and reporting we need for our ideas.

'Leadership is mainly required in my *sphere of influence,* where I can volunteer to improve and change things. I may need to break some rules in the sphere of influence, where they are not achieving the results we want, and show initiative. Rather than being a victim of the systems and processes in the business, I may need to work with my team to change and improve some of them.

'Chris, you are 100% correct, and remember you first have to master the rules before you can break them.'

'Great point,' Chris said. 'Leadership is all about change. It starts with being dissatisfied with the status quo - having constructive discontent.'

'You will find your team is very good at that part.' Sonya smiled.

'Too true,' said Chris. 'I remember my previous manager making the mistake of asking the team to list all the problems they could see. We ran out of space on the whiteboard.'

Sonya took her chance to find out more about the previous manager, so she had context on Chris's sudden appointment. 'Chris, do you know why your previous manager left so suddenly?'

'Yes, I do know. She was fired. I had tried to warn her that she should tell our management how bad things had become, but she said management only wanted to hear good news.

'Everyone loved her as she was a real *people* person, but she had no idea what any of us did, and she never got involved in anything, always telling us she didn't want to interfere. She did not interact with customers either. We had several serious customer issues and were missing our targets. She never reported any of this, always hoping for a miracle. The miracle never happened, and her world came crashing around her feet once management realised how bad things were.'

Chris shook his head solemnly, then smiled confidently. 'I like this quote from the textbook, "once you have identified the problems, to display leadership, you also have to volunteer to be part of the solution."

'Be a *change agent*.' Chris continued. 'A leadership mindset is the opposite of a *victim* mindset. A victim refuses to get involved and blames others for the status quo. My previous manager blamed her management and even our customers for all our problems. She always put us first, but sometimes I think the balance was wrong. What I am hoping to do differently is to be part of the solution and not blame anyone else for our situation.'

'Wonderful, Chris. I am so thrilled that you picked up on this critical aspect of leadership. This is true for your team, and remember, it is also true for you. When you lick your wounds and blame everyone around you for your problems, you display a victim mindset rather than a leadership mindset. What else did you learn?'

'I liked the point that leadership requires a culture of continuous learning. They quoted Microsoft CEO Satya Nadella, who said, "*Learn it all* will always do better than *know it all*." I'm going to use that quote. It's a great way of reminding my team of what a leadership mindset looks like.'

'You are displaying a leadership mindset right now by embracing these new ideas. Please go on.'

'Leaders are more forward-looking than backwards-looking. The only point of looking backwards is to learn how to do something better in the future.'

'Remember that,' said Sonya, 'when your management asks you to report on what went wrong. Balance the management activities with a leadership mindset that focuses on the future.'

'Good advice,' Chris replied. 'The last thing that stood out for me when looking at the leadership mindset was that leaders create a positive and empowering environment. I found it interesting to read that empowerment is not effective without boundaries. Management sets up processes and systems to achieve repeatable results, allowing empowerment to flourish within those boundaries. My job is not to tell my team how to do their jobs, but to allow them autonomous freedom, and to do that, I need to establish governance.'

'Well done, Chris. You are getting to grips with what is required to lead a team. Remember I am away in Paris next week for the annual trade show. I will meet with you the following week.'

On Friday morning, Chris went over to the coffee shop and got deeply engrossed in his book. A loud noise distracted him. Without him realising it, the staff had packed up the surrounding chairs, ready to go home. An internal meeting was taking place behind the counter, and a new manager was addressing the small team. The barista had a pained expression on his face while this young manager explained to him exactly how he wanted everything set up.

'Please only use the cups with the new logo, and I want you to use the new coffee beans with our new menu.'

'Yes, we know,' the barista said. 'We have been planning the new menu for months, and I was the one who recommended the new coffee beans. We were involved in tasting all the options for the new menu.'

The manager continued. 'It's *really* important that you learn the new menu and only use the new cups and coffee beans. Please stack the cups *here*.'

'We know!' they all shouted back in unison.

'I am all about quality,' said the manager. 'Customer experience is everything. I want to make sure that you treat each cup of coffee as a piece of art.'

The team stared at the floor gloomily. Eventually, the barista said, 'Listen, I have been making coffee here for over four years, and my customers love me. You have been a manager here for exactly one week. Why don't you do your job, and I will do mine?'

The rest of the team, also irritated by the pep talk, asked if the meeting was over and if they could go home.

Chris could see the enthusiasm dissipate in the new manager and saw where he was going wrong, but he felt sorry for him. He paid for his coffee and left with his textbook under his arm, thinking, 'Managing skilled people is not easy.'

THE BIRTH OF SCIENTIFIC MANAGEMENT

Sonya opened her eyes and rushed over to the window to draw back the curtains of her hotel room. There in the distance was one of the world's most famous icons - the Eiffel tower. She felt disappointed. Compared to the image she had built up in her head about how it would look, considering it was over 300m high, it seemed somewhat small and unimposing. That was not the only thing that was small. Her hotel room, while quaint, was the size of a matchbox, and she had struggled to sleep on the rather small hotel bed, especially while feeling jet lagged. What wasn't small was the price. She stretched out her arms, trying to be positive and proclaimed, 'I am in Paris.' She pinched her arm playfully. 'I am in Paris!'

Sonya was in Paris for the annual World Fair, which was established in 1889. The 1900 Paris Exposition World Fair was considered one of the most impressive fairs of all time and opened its doors to more than 50 million people over seven months. One display amongst the over 80,000 exhibitors was by Bethlehem Steel, displaying their High-Speed Steel Exhibit. The creator of this system was Frederick Winslow Taylor, born in the American city of Philadelphia in 1856. Taylor was highly intelligent, and when he passed the Harvard entrance exam with honours, everyone assumed he would follow in his father's footsteps, who was a Princeton educated lawyer. Concerns about his health led to him dropping out of college, and he went to work in a machine shop doing mechanical engineering work. What Taylor saw in the workplace appalled him, and he spent the rest of his career challenging the status quo to transform the workplace. While at Bethlehem Steel, Taylor took his high-speed steel cutting system over to the World Fair to show the world how engineering should be done.

The organisers of the current World Fair had recreated Taylor's exhibit and had hired people to dress up in period clothes and answer questions about his ideas and systems.

Sonya wiped the crumbs away from her mouth as she devoured the most delicious croissant she had ever tasted, but compared to American coffee, she found the Cappuccino strong and bitter and wondered if there was a Starbucks nearby. After spending a few minutes trying to figure out the currency conversion to see how much she had actually paid for her meal, she placed some Euro notes on her table. She hoped that the tip from the change would not be insulting to the very professional waiter that had served her breakfast. With that, she headed to the show.

As she walked down the tree-lined avenue of the Champs Elysees and through the Arc de Triomphe, she viewed the Eiffel Tower in a different light. In context, it was impressive, and she vowed to go to the top after spending the day at the conference centre. When she walked into the exhibition hall and found the Taylor stand, a man was enthusiastically explaining how his mini factory was transforming the industry. Dressed in a tweed jacket with a matching waistcoat and smart collar, he wore a tie fastened in the style of a man working in a practical occupation rather than how a banker or lawyer would dress.

He was holding a copy of *The principles of scientific management* and waving it around in the way a preacher would use the bible. A continuity director would have taken issue with adding this prop in the scene.

Frederick Taylor only wrote the book after he retired in 1911, and the great Paris Exhibition was in the year 1900. Sonya let it pass as poetic license.

The man continued his sermon. 'In the past, *the man* has been first; in the future, *the system* must be first. In the past, the theory has been that if we could get the right man, methods could be safely left to him. In the future, it will be appreciated that no *great* man can compete with ordinary men who have been properly and efficiently organised. These principles of scientific management apply to all kinds of human activities.'

Sonya cringed at the sexist language but considered that women only entered the workplace after World War two, long after Taylor's time.

Someone shouted out, grinning devilishly while keeping the paid actor in character. 'Mr Taylor, your cutting machine is very impressive but give us evidence that this system really applies to other areas of life outside engineering.'

The actor, relishing his role as Taylor, smiled back broadly and offered the evidence. 'Well, I applied my efficiency model to playing tennis, and 20 years ago, my cousin and I won the US National Championships for the men's doubles. I apply this model to all areas of my life. I've even perfected the process to make scrambled eggs.'

A hand shot up. 'Mr Taylor, what would you say is the heart of your message today, other than the ingenious and efficient machinery on show?'

'Firstly, the fallacy has been that a material increase in work would result in throwing a large number of men out of work. Secondly, the defective systems of management make it necessary for a workman to *soldier*.'

Sonya wasn't sure what he meant by *soldier*. She was not alone. The actor picked up that his audience did not understand this term and added some ad-lib comments.

'For my British visitors, I believe you call this "hanging it out." Soldiering is when workers deliberately do as little as they can safely do. Isn't it odd that the same worker, when playing sport, strains every nerve to secure victory and would be considered a quitter if they did any less, and yet at work, the goal is to do as little as they can get away with.' The actor looked satisfied that he had defined the term in the way Taylor would have replied.

'The third key element of my model is that inefficient rule-of-thumb methods that all our workers deploy need to be replaced by "one-best-way using scientific methods."'

Sonya's mind wandered back to the present time. As she had read Taylor's book, she could tell the actor was quoting verbatim from it. She wandered away to the rest of the stand and marvelled at the level of detail that Taylor had gone into to define his efficiency model. The stand showcased process-flow charts and detailed instructions to workers. Photographs of managers using time-and-motion studies to analyse the workflow were also on display. Taylor's system demanded that they equally divided the factory workers between the managers who planned the work and the workers who executed those plans. The work had to be done without deviation from the plan.

'Isn't it interesting?' Sonya thought. 'This model virtually single-handedly transformed the way industry operated, resulting in the Industrial Revolution.'

Sonya read on one of the display boards that Henry Ford had applied Taylor's model to the car chassis assembly of his Model T motor vehicles post-1900. This reduced the production time from 13 ½ hours to 1 hour. 'Imagine reporting those efficiency results in your annual review,' Sonya remarked under her breath.

She spent the rest of the day examining all the various displays and, despite her interest in the topic, eventually took a cab back to her hotel, where she freshened up and went off to venture to the top of the Eiffel tower. Paris looked so magical that she had to wrench herself away as she remembered she had a meeting planned with Pierre Leroux, Chris's team member.

When Sonya arrived at the cafe, Pierre had already secured a table for them sitting outside, and he seemed a lot more positive and charming than Chris had described him.

'Where are you staying?' Pierre asked.

'Hotel Montpellier.'

'Oh, that is fantastic. Did you know that place was originally built in the 17th century and was only recently restored? A very famous local carpenter did the artwork embedded in the wood panelling. Have you tried the wine? They have a fabulous selection of Pinot Noir wines from the region that they named the hotel after. At least they didn't put you up in something characterless like the Hilton.'

Sonya thought about how she hadn't even noticed all the positive aspects of the hotel, as she had been so focused on the small size of her room and bed and secretly had longed for a bigger room at the Hilton, but she let it pass. As they discussed the work situation, it soon became apparent that Pierre was very engaged with the company and committed to the team's success but felt excluded.

'Team conference calls are often late in the day, where it is already dinner time here. I am seen as negative and impatient when I complain about the calls that drag on late into the night. They use the whiteboard extensively and never consider that I cannot see what they are writing. I always feel like a less important team member because I am not physically in the office with them. I hope that Chris and I can work together collaboratively, but I must admit it wasn't a good start when I found out by email that Chris was appointed as the manager, and he never called me to tell me.'

Sonya moved the conversation onto other matters, and after an hour, they parted company.

Meanwhile, back in America, it was early afternoon. Chris looked at his watch and realised that he was late for a team catch-up on a critical project. The team was enthusiastically engaged in discussing the project and reported that everything was on track. Chris asked his team to provide details and noticed that Emily, the newest member of his team, was using different presentation software to the one he was used to. This made it harder for Chris to understand the report.

'Emily, please can you redo this project plan using the software we normally use? It is taking me longer to understand this report because I am not used to this layout.'

Fred, one of the experienced team members, challenged Chris. He pointed out that the current software that the team was using was out of date. Emily's software improved the overall reporting. All the other stakeholders loved it.

Chris felt irritated but couldn't think of a good reason to oppose it, other than it made his life harder. He was also currently busy working on upgrading the project scheduling software and didn't want to investigate another software change. He felt he was losing control. 'Emily, when you have as much experience as I do, you can choose new software for the department. In the meantime, please use the software that I have provided.'

Chris left the meeting feeling dejected. He had won the battle but felt terrible inside. 'I wish Sonya was here.' Chris groaned. 'I still don't think I get whether I am the boss that can make decisions or whether I am the cheerleader for the team.'

A NEW PARADIGM IN MANAGEMENT

On her last day in Paris, Sonya visited a French electronics company called *J. R. Dupont and Sons.* James Jackson, the CEO, was American and had asked to meet, as she had done some coaching with a colleague of his who had recommended her.

Still privately owned, *Dupont,* as it was known in the industry, had been in business for 50 years and had a good reputation for high-quality and reliable products, but in recent years had fallen behind in innovation. James had a long history of developing start-up companies to a point where they received external funding. His most recent business turnaround story had made the business pages of the New York Times. The Dupont family had read about James's successes in America and convinced him to move to Paris and accept the role as CEO, to see if he could turn his magic hand to growing and expanding their solid, but slow growth company.

James was convinced he had cracked the code to industrial progress. His solution was to undo everything Taylor had done 100 years prior. James had been warned that Sonya was a fan of Taylor, which confused him as she also had a reputation for supporting empowered leadership for all. He was looking forward to a good debate.

Sonya arrived at James' office, and they walked together to the boardroom. 'Hi Sonya, thanks for meeting with me.'

'Hi James, pleased to meet you. I have heard good things about you.'

'Please call me Jim. Your reputation precedes you as well. Let me give you some background on why I asked to see you. Dupont is at the cutting edge of technology. The minimum qualifications that our workers have is a master's degree. We believe that our success is all about innovation. At Dupont, we run the business on teamwork, and we abhor process and structure. We need to be nimble and flexible. We threw our job descriptions out the window and have eliminated the departmental silos. In Dupont, we want people to think about the end customer and not focus internally. Everyone is equal, and everyone is empowered. Dupont has no middle management layers. We treat our staff as adults and have figured out that the *workers* are king. If we treat our workers as king, they will treat the customers as king, and then the financial results will give the shareholders the returns they are looking for. Our role as senior managers is to support and inspire our teams so they can excel. Dupont won an award this year for "most inspiring company to work for."'

Sonya guessed that this was a well-practised narrative.

'That sounds fantastic.' She paused and then added. 'If everything is going so well, why do you want to see me?'

The CEO looked down as though she had caught him stealing ice cream from the fridge while on a diet. He picked up his pen and doodled as he collected his thoughts.

'To be honest, things are not turning out as well as I would like. I had a clean sheet of paper and a large pot of money to spend in my start-up companies. Here, I have existing customers to look after, and the operating profits fund my Research and Development. Our people are happy and motivated, but we also find that their commitment to customers is not as high as we would expect. Some people are taking the flexibility and empowerment that we offer and abusing it for personal gain.

'Our engineering teams are full of great ideas, but not enough products are actually getting out to market to give us the financial results we need. Our investors are tiring of propping up our R&D budget with no returns. We are great at starting things but not good at finishing them.

'Everybody is involved, and everybody feels empowered, but nobody is sure who owns the issue when things go wrong. I've realised that because *everybody* owns the issue, *nobody* owns the issue, and so it ends up on my desk to resolve. I don't have the expertise to fix the issue, and I have relinquished my authority in an inverted leadership model, and so I feel powerless to enforce the changes we need.

'My first year here I wandered around the organisation demanding that we break down the silos, but now that we have this flat structure, I wish I had them again, as at least I knew who owned the various functional aspects.'

Jim looked dejected. Sonya knew from his impressive resume that he was no fool. She also knew from talking to people that he was an imposing personality that was both feared and respected. Sonya had seen this play out in so many dynamic, technology-driven companies. She smiled warmly and looked up at Jim.

'You are not alone in wanting clarity on functional responsibility. Yesterday, I went to the World Trade fair at the exhibition centre, where they had a stand showcasing Taylor's manufacturing methods. The reason that Taylor's methods revolutionised the world in terms of efficiency is that they worked.'

'But Sonya, they don't work. When I first arrived here, everyone worked inside their silos and gave themselves clean scorecards, yet our customers were not happy, and therefore our shareholders were not happy. Processes slow everything down and stifle creativity. Traditional managers think they are in charge, so they make decisions without understanding the consequences of their decisions. The engineers knew these management decisions were wrong but were powerless to intervene because of the org structure.'

He picked up a diagram off his table. Sonya recognised it as the

Inverted leadership model, but she feigned ignorance. 'Sonya, there is a new management paradigm. I cannot go back to a Taylor model.' He laid the inverted leadership model down in front of Sonya.

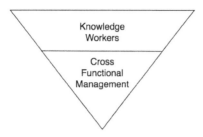

'The late Peter Drucker realised that the modern smart workforce are no longer *uneducated* Taylor workers. Drucker called them *knowledge* workers, and he said that today's workers are the executives of the past. I agree with that. My employees know more about their jobs than I do.

'Facebook's Julie Zhuo, in her book *The making of a manager*, says that the role of a manager "is not to do the work yourself, even if you are the best at it, because that will only take you so far. Your role is to improve the purpose, people, and process of your team to get as high a multiplier effect on your collective outcome as you can."

'My role and that of my management team are to support these smart knowledge workers to get the right business outcomes. Taylor didn't want workers to think. The principal thing I want from my workforce is thinking.'

Sonya was seeing evidence of the tough, steely personality that others had warned her about.

'Jim, the *Taylor model* works where the end result is known in advance. The *inverted leadership model* works when the end result is not known in advance. Taylor understood that efficient execution is achieved by separating the thinker-phase from the doer-phase. The challenge in a modern organisation is that we have to run two completely opposite management structures concurrently. We need the knowledge workers to operate in an inverted leadership model and create new processes and structure to achieve scalable outputs. We must reunite the *planning* and the *doing* activities into one smart worker, whereas in the past, we had supervisory managers doing the thinking and work-to-rule workers doing the execution.

'Let's look at innovation. The very definition of innovation means that you cannot know in advance what the outcome is. Setting up a Taylor factory with the associated Taylor mindset will stifle creative thinking and slow down progress. On the other hand, the need to have a final "product" to come out of the creative thinking process at a predetermined time with a predetermined value is no different to Taylor's day where a production line existed. Innovation without an innovation *process* is not likely to yield predictable business outcomes. In the processless chaos of start-up companies, occasionally someone hits the jackpot. Business schools love to quote the story about the designer at 3M, who had failed to produce a super strong glue. His failed product had resulted in one of the most successful products in history - the sticky notes.

'The problem is that the story is from 1968. If that was a repeatable model, we could quote a lot more recent examples that would support the idea that chaotic, processless innovation is the desired business model. Even Google is now downplaying the importance of their *20% Rule* program, where staff could work on anything they liked, and which supposedly created *Gmail* - one of their most successful products. The current Google managers are quick to point out that what is more important is the *80% Rule*, where 80% of their focus needs to be on fully released, sellable products. In fact, Paul Buchheit, *Gmail's* creator, dispels the myth that Gmail was a random invention, saying that it was a planned project from the beginning. The Taylor model and the Inverted Leadership model go hand-in-hand.'

'Interesting Sonya, very interesting. In my previous businesses, I have always had managers around me who introduced Taylor-style governance, and my style has always been inverted leadership. I now realise that it was the *balance* between the two models that achieved my past successes.'

Jim thanked Sonya for her time and offered his opinion that this may well be the breakthrough in his thinking that would help to transform this half-century-old business. They both stood up. 'Sonya, next time you're in Paris I'd love to meet up again.'

Sonya thanked Jim and made her way to the airport for her long journey home. As the taxi driver raced in slow motion through the over-crowded roads, narrowly avoiding a crash on numerous occasions, she reflected on her week. Sonya hoped her time spent in Paris could help with her assignment with Chris.

She closed her eyes and prayed she would not end up with a middle seat on her long flight back to America.

A TEAM IN DISARRAY

It was still Friday morning in America, and Chris was sitting in on a project meeting. He was pleased with how well the team members were getting along socially. They all had great attitudes, but in their enthusiasm, people were tripping up over each other.

'I've completed the schedule,' said Fred proudly.

'Why didn't you tell me you were doing that?' Madison complained. 'I spent half of last night doing exactly the same task.'

'Well, I was trying to be helpful.'

'I appreciate that, Fred, but I thought it was my role to do the schedule.'

'We are all a team, aren't we? Who has updated the customer with the latest project delay?'

The team looked around at each other guiltily and then looked across at Chris, hoping he would help clarify whose job it was to do that.

Following his rather unsatisfactory intervention about the software the previous day, Chris decided not to interfere this time and left the team arguing round and round in circles, hoping they would figure it all out.

Chris realised he had not handled recent meetings well but was not sure what to do. He was looking forward to Sonya arriving and discussing how to develop his management skills.

The following week, Chris met up with Sonya in a spare meeting room at the office. 'So, how was your trip?' Chris asked. 'Did you catch up with Pierre?'

'It was great,' Sonya replied. 'I had some interesting experiences, and yes, I met Pierre.'

'I suppose he had lots of complaints about me?'

'Well, it does seem he feels a bit left out of the team communication. We can work on that in the coming weeks.'

Chris smiled wryly. 'I meant to call him to tell him about my role. I ran out of time.'

'Did you run out of time, or had you decided it was not a priority to tell him?'

'Of course it was a priority, but Pierre is always so negative. I kept procrastinating because I knew it was not going to be a fun call.'

'Chris, have you considered that your reluctance to involve him in things may be causing a vicious circle? I didn't get the impression from him that he has any issues with your leadership, other than that you exclude him.'

As Chris reflected on her statement, Sonya moved the topic on. 'How were things here? What have you learnt about leadership?'

'Okay, here goes.' Chris said. 'This is how I understand it so far. The work itself has become too complex for a manager to know or understand exactly what to do or how to do it. Managers can certainly prescribe best practice in terms of standards, look and feel, and brand, but the steps to achieve those outputs are usually better left to the staff who are actually doing the job.' Chris looked at Sonya, conscious that he was on a roll and wanted to be sure she approved.

'Go on. I like what I'm hearing.'

'Okay, thanks. For my team, most of their activities require them to figure out the *how*. My role is to help clarify what *results* to expect rather than enforce the "one right way." My team isn't expected to follow my orders. They plan and manage their own work. They control what they do, how they do it and when they do it. Taylor figured out how to get work done efficiently, but he also separated the *planning* and *doing* roles. Today, the worker needs to take on both roles. Initially, they are the *manager,* and then they switch hats and become the *worker* to their own management plans.

'I need to support my team. I am not really the boss, except for those compliance issues, like timesheets and leave forms and HR disciplines. My team members are not lugging pig iron across a factory floor, like in Taylor's day. If I want to get the best out of these smart people, I need to let them do both the *thinking* and *doing* part of the role. I am not expected to have all the answers, nor am I the only one to initiate process improvements. My role is to share the business goals and then support the team in figuring out what process improvements they can think of, to achieve the business goals.'

Sonya was impressed with Chris's insights about his manager role, but she had heard about the earlier meeting and was keen to address the issue.

'Chris, last week, when you met with your team, I heard there was a lot of confusion about roles and responsibilities. The one person who has the authority to define those roles is you. In terms of the work itself, the team members may indeed have better insights on what must be done, but the team interfaces and responsibilities need to be set initially by yourself. Team members do not want their managers interfering in things they already know how to do, but they do want their managers assisting in things that are outside their control.'

'Thanks, Sonya. On reflection, I abdicated my management role to save face. An incident happened while you were away. I became impatient with a team member for not seeing things my way. Emily was using new software for the project reporting that everyone loved, except me. I am embarrassed to say that when I wrapped up the conversation, I said, "When you have as much experience as I do, you can choose your own software. In the meantime, do it my way, please."

Chris looked despondent as this event played out in his mind. 'Sonya,

I have gone over and over in my head why I acted so out of character, and I think the reason is I still have a conflict between empowering my team and being the boss. I like my team being empowered when they do things my way, but when they come up with things I disagree with, I find myself wanting to be in charge again. I will definitely look into that new presentation software to understand why other people seem to like it, but I am so frustrated with myself for behaving that way.'

'Chris, this is a long-term journey, so don't beat yourself up for making mistakes so long as you are learning.'

'Sonya, I am learning, but this is hard.'

'It is hard. Do not underestimate the complexity of the new role you have taken on. The leadership challenges that you face when managing a small team of people apply to senior leadership roles. Learning how to be a good team leader is excellent training for becoming the CEO of a company.'

Sonya smiled, and with a wave of her hand, left the meeting room.

Chris rose slowly and headed back to his office. Tomorrow was another day. Today he had 101 problems to solve, and he almost regretted the time he had spent thinking about leadership, as he was even further behind in solving these operational issues. He picked up his phone and called home.

'Sorry darling, I have no choice but to work late tonight. In some ways, I blame this new leadership coach. She has given me so much extra stuff to read and think about that it has delayed me finishing the real work that I must do. My team has not been particularly helpful either as they keep bringing me problems to solve that I think they could handle themselves. My boss is also dumping a lot of extra stuff on me with no consideration for how busy I already am. Anyway, my new leadership coach says I must not become a victim. Easy for her to say, she doesn't have a real job like me. I think if I put in a couple of extra hours tonight, I can get ahead of things again. Start dinner without me, and I will try to be home before the kids go to sleep. I promise next week will be different.'

DEFINING TEAMWORK

It was the weekend, and Chris was at the Grand Prix. He was a lifelong lover of Formula One racing. Chris was fascinated - not only by the experience of being deafened by the noise of the cars racing around the track at speeds exceeding 200 miles per hour - but also by the incredible teamwork involved in the race.

Formula One cars are engineered to the sheer limits of modern technology. Costing millions of dollars each, the car's acceleration exceeds that of a small plane taking off. Aerodynamic down-forces are required to keep the cars from becoming airborne. Drivers experience forces of 5G as they accelerate at a mind-numbing pace and race into hairpin bends. The driver can lose up to 5 kg of weight through water loss in a single race. The tyre tread gets worn down too and so needs to be changed at regular intervals. Mid-race refuelling is a controversial safety issue and has been alternatively allowed or banned every decade or so.

Chris watched in awe as a car raced into the pits, stopped abruptly and over a dozen team members rushed into action in perfect unison to stabilise the vehicle, change four tyres, plus complete a myriad of technical adjustments, all in under three seconds. The conductor of this flawless performance is the so-called *lollipop man*. Nowadays, this is mostly done with electronic signalling. Still, historically as the most senior member of the team, the lollipop man was the team leader that jumps out in front of the car in the pits as it races to a grinding halt with his lollipop - a reference to the red sign on the end of a pole.

The lollipop man lets the driver know when he can move on, in addition to supervising the entire process. The signalling tells the driver when to apply brakes, when to engage first gear, and when to depart. The lollipop man controls the timings and is responsible for the safety in the pit. Yet, he does not actually issue any instructions to team members or directly control the detail of the work activities. How could he? The entire process happens in the blink of an eye. The pit stop crew chief commands a million-dollar salary, as races are often won or lost based on pit stop performance.

Performing activities in the blink of an eye are so stressful that the team members' heart rates race to above 160 bpm. Losing one-tenth of a second in the pits could make all the difference to a podium position. Training for mechanics is akin to that of an elite athlete. The driver is the star of the show but winning is a team effort.

Chris thought about his challenge of building a high-performance team at work. The recent team meeting had been anything but a team of people working in perfect unison. Most of the team had no clear idea of their roles, nor did they have clarity on their unique contribution to the team. Teamwork in Chris's company seemed to be measured by how well everyone got along socially and whether they did their work in a group setting rather than working independently.

Chris decided to talk to Sonya about it on Monday. He was brought back to the present as a car spectacularly crashed into a barrier. It brought back memories of the death of his childhood hero, Brazilian Ayrton Senna, in 1994. The crash was a harsh reminder of how dangerous this sport was, but he secretly enjoyed the drama and excitement. He justified it morally on the basis that these days fatalities were so rare. The cars had incredible safety features, and a Formula One helmet is subject to some of the harshest tests on the planet. The driver got out of the car shaken but unhurt, as another army of marshals, medics, firefighters, and officials worked with military precision to check on his well-being, activate the safety procedures and flag the danger to other cars in the race.

When Chris got home and had finished sharing his excitement for the race in a lap-by-lap commentary, he settled down to read his *Leader's guide* book.

WHAT IS A TEAM?

A team is not just a crowd or a collection of individuals with a common interest. A team is also more than just a group. A group benefits from synergy. Synergy comes from the Greek word *synergia*, which means "joint work and cooperative action." It is where the joint outcome is more than the sum of the parts.

Consider geese. When gathered on the ground, milling about honking aimlessly, they are a group or a gaggle. But when they decide to fly somewhere specific, they become a team, united by a task-oriented purpose. According to an article published in *Science* magazine in May 1970, called *Formation Flight of Birds*, by Lissaman and Shollenberger, a V-formation of 25 birds can achieve a reduction of induced drag by up to 65%, and as a result, increase their range by approximately 70%. By working together as a team, rotating leadership, and honking encouragement to one another, the geese achieve far more than an individual goose achieves on its own. Teamwork is more than having a common interest or being in close proximity. Teams exist to achieve a specific output.

A group may benefit from synergy, but a team is formed for a specific and task-oriented purpose. A group of people may don the same shirts and travel together to a football game and be united by their allegiance to the football club. But, they only become a team if they decide to unite behind a particular activity.

There is a mistaken belief in the workplace that teamwork is all about having a good attitude towards other team members and doing things together. Teamwork is far more than that. In fact, the least efficient way to get something done is often to do it as a group exercise.

Group exercises are often enjoyed by extroverts who are ener-gised by interacting with people. Talking with others helps them to form their own ideas. Enjoying the interaction and talking together does not always contribute to the task at hand. Working as a group can lead to social loafing, where freeloaders shirk their responsibil-ities. Evaluation apprehension or the fear of looking stupid in front of others can create groupthink which can stifie performance. The other thing that can stifie performance is production blocking. In a group exercise, only one person can speak at a time. Many studies have shown that idea generation, while working alone prior to sharing ideas, can produce higher quality ideas than when produced in a group setting. Human beings are conformist by nature and so heavily infiuenced by other people's ideas and decisions.

For teams to be highly effective, a clear distinction needs to be made on when and how team members work as a group and when they need to work alone. Studies have shown open-plan offices and teams working in groups can reduce productivity and even impair memory.

Chris recalled a group assignment that he had done as part of his MBA. He had met with his fellow students after work to review progress on an assignment. One person in the group was an accountant and had taken the lead on the case study to analyse the business metrics for a fictitious company. Six people sat in a circle watching the accountant work, with the occasional word of encouragement or admonishment to work faster. In reality, only one person was doing the actual work, and the others were adding no value. The purpose of doing the exercise as a group assignment was for everybody to be involved, provide opinions, and contribute. The reality turned out to be very different.

Chris thought to himself. 'When it comes down to the work itself, I think it is far better to divvy the work up and give it to individuals. There were over a dozen people in the pit stop team, and everyone had their own role. Teamwork is about working together, but it is also about working as individuals.' He paused and said, 'Another one of Sonya's contradictions,' then kept reading.

VIRTUAL TEAMS

Many teams have team members that do not report to the same line manager. Virtual teams are geographically dispersed and consist of a range of stakeholders, including temporary workers, contractors and even suppliers.

In the book, *Virtual Teams* (2000), Lipnack and Stamps define a virtual team as 'a group of people who work interdependently, with shared purpose across space, time and organisational boundaries using technology.'

The research shows that where teams are physically separated by more than the size of a basketball court, collaboration *increases* the further away the teams are physically situated. Paradoxically, a team in another country or state is likely to have more collaboration between its team members than a team spread out in the same building by more than 50 feet. The reason for this absurdity is that when people are located far away from each other, it is obvious they cannot collaborate physically. When they are in close proximity but not close enough to interact, there is a perception that collaboration is occurring, but in practice, it does not happen.

Virtual teams need to set up specific communication and collaboration methods to simulate the teamwork naturally experienced by sharing a physical space. Video conferencing, chat rooms, shared information boards and opportunities for non-work-related social interaction need to be planned to simulate what happens when human beings interact in close proximity.

◆　◆　◆

Chris reflected on Sonya's feedback about Pierre. He was on the other side of the world, yet Chris had neglected to set things up to allow Pierre to collaborate as an equal team member. He committed to fixing that. With the travel restrictions introduced during the COVID pandemic, even local team members had learnt to meet remotely rather than face-to-face. Chris realised he had work to do to create an interactive, collaborative environment for *all* team members. Sonya had also recommended that where several people dial in, he should get *everyone* in the group to join online. She had said. 'There is nothing worse than being a fly on the wall watching everyone else socialise in a face-to-face setting while you watch on from your computer.' Chris read on.

CLARITY OF OWNERSHIP

Teams require joint ownership and commitment to a successful outcome, but they also require individual and unique ownership relating to their role within the team. Each team member needs to understand the difference between inputs, activities, suppliers, and outputs to ensure their individual contribution achieves the desired joint outcome. The customer (external or internal) is the person or department that the deliverables are handed to. Teams that are not end-customer-focused end up focusing instead on team activities and busyness that may, or may not, result in overall business value.

◆　◆　◆

Chris tried to relate this to what he had seen at the Grand Prix. The people changing tyres were critical to the success of the pit stop. Chris recalled the thrilling Monaco Grand Prix in 2016 when Australian Red

Bull driver Daniel Ricciardo who had pole position, lost to British world champion Lewis Hamilton when his tyres were not ready for him in the pitstop. A last-minute change to the plan of which tyres to use led to confusion with the team members, costing the driver a podium position.

A pit stop team works as a team, but they also work as individuals. Each person knows their role and works on their own to do the task itself. They also know the timing of when their contribution fits into the overall picture. Understanding how and when each component fits into the overall picture is a critical element of teamwork.

In Chris's operational team model, the *customer* is the driver of the car. The *input* is the driver arriving at the pit stop, which triggers the request to change the tyres. From that second onwards, the tyre changers are on a timer for their role in the race. The *supplier* is the person providing them with the right tyre at the right time. The team must manage that *interface,* in addition to the task at hand. The *activity* is to change the tyre. The details of the tyre-changing activity are of no interest to people outside the tyre-changing team. Other team members and the end-customer are interested in the *output* - the *deliverable* - a changed tyre.

Chris reached for his notebook and drew a diagram:

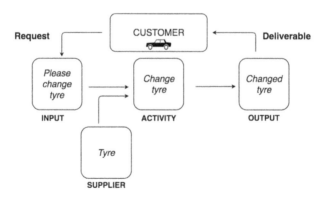

Chris studied what he had drawn carefully. 'I think this model will help me define *ownership* for multi-departmental activities and help me define customer-driven measures instead of silo-centric measures. I must discuss this more with Sonya.'

STAGES OF TEAMWORK

Chris tucked his book under his arm and walked down to the kitchen to pour himself a glass of wine. He then settled into his favourite chair in the lounge and continued reading.

STAGES OF TEAM DEVELOPMENT

In 1965, Bruce Tuckman defined four stages of team development: Forming, storming, norming and performing. Tuckman stressed that teams needed to be formally established with strong direction from the team leader. Inevitably, teams would then go into a confiict phase as the team members challenged the way things were set up. Constructive confiict, and more involvement from the team members to challenge the way the team is set up, allows teams to progress to a norming phase where they operate well as a team. To become a high-performance team, the role of the team leader would become less directive as the leadership aspects were distributed between team members.

❖ ❖ ❖

Chris then read a summary of *The One Minute Manager builds high-performance teams,* by Ken Blanchard (2004). He also read about *The Five Dysfunctions of a team,* by Patrick Lencioni (2016). He noticed many similarities between the various team stages in these different models. He realised that the reason a lot of self-directed team initiatives had failed in the past was that there was no phased team development.

Chris put down the book and reflected on his team. He had been nervous about being seen as an old-fashioned Taylor-styled manager and preferred the image of an empowering leader. He realised they could not become a high-performance team before he defined the roles and team outputs.

Chris's team members were all very experienced in the actual job, but the team had never actually developed as a combined unit. He realised he needed to start from scratch and actually re-establish *the team.*

Despite how long everyone had worked together, they were effectively in the Forming (establishment) stage. Chris realised he needed to be prescriptive in the required outputs, roles, structure, and communication methods. He also needed to define the *why* rather than the *what* to get buy-in and alignment of the team's goals.

Chris then took out his notebook and summarised in his own words the phases he knew the team would need to go through as it matured over the coming months:

- ◆ **Phase 1** *(Establishment)*
  - ○ *Directive style*
  - ○ *Define roles*
  - ○ *Create structure*
  - ○ *Define reporting and communication required*
  - ○ *Clarify the difference between activities and outputs (deliverables)*
  - ○ *Identify the customer and customer measures*
  - ○ *Build team relationships*
  - ○ *Focus on "the why"*

- ***Phase 2*** *(Alignment)*
    - ○ *Make it safe for the team to challenge the setup*
    - ○ *Ask the team what is working and what is not working*
    - ○ *Encourage team participation*
    - ○ *Allow and encourage constructive conflict*
- ***Phase 3*** *(Commitment)*
    - ○ *"We before me" - team affiliation comes first*
    - ○ *Move to a supportive role to optimise performance*
    - ○ *Distribute leadership functions*
    - ○ *Raise the bar*
- ***Phase 4*** *(Autonomy)*
    - ○ *Fully empower the team*
    - ○ *Stay connected*

Chris continued reading his book.

THE ORGANISATIONAL STRUCTURE OF TEAMS

In the workplace, two types of teams exist. **Functional teams**, defined by the official organisational structure, and **dynamic cross-functional teams**, established to complete a particular task or project. John Kotter, in his book *Accelerate* (2014), has an excellent theoretical description that defines how these teams need to be set up and how they must coexist within one organisation.

Kotter says that the functional team structure is "based on the traditional hierarchies and managerial processes," and cross-functional teams are "an agile, network-like structure and a very different set of processes."

Semi-permanent functional teams are useful in a stable environment, where it is well known what needs to be done, and the environment is stable. Traditional management processes achieve compliance to predetermined standards.

The challenge of a modern business is that the process and

activities to achieve the end goal are not specifically known by the managers. Even if the methods *were* known, the environment changes so fast that the method may be rendered outmoded.

Innovation, for example, is hard to define, and by its very nature, the solution is unknown at the start of the process. The solution is discovered during the process, and so it is unclear what specific milestones or quality metrics should be insisted upon by the manager. Managers cannot drive and direct teams to achieve things that the managers themselves are unclear about. In these circumstances, performance is achieved through people who are intrinsically motivated.

In his book *Drive: The surprising truth about what motivates us* (2009), Daniel Pink argues that trying to motivate those people through the traditional carrot-stick approach is counterproductive.

Kotter calls these people *volunteers*, "You cannot mobilise voluntary energy and brainpower unless people want to be change agents and feel they have permission to do so. The spirit of volunteerism - the desire to work with others for a shared purpose - energises the network."

Dual structures are required: Formal structures, with authority limits and organisation charts; and agile structures, with cross-functional teams, who understand the vision, have a deep commitment to seeing the business succeed and understand what leadership is all about.

Chris put the book down and frowned. He was not sure he understood the significance of Kotter's model.

Chris applied it to his team. 'So, I am the manager, and I suppose that is part of the traditional hierarchical structure. I know what the team is set up for and that *my* manager expects me to deliver known business results. These outputs have been defined in terms of Key Performance Indicators (KPI's).

'So, what is this parallel structure that Kotter is referring to? Each of my team members ends up on cross-functional teams and various corporate initiatives. It drives me crazy that those activities distract them, but I suppose they are needed for these voluntary groups from the company's perspective. I had never thought before that they are not operating under the formal HR structure of the business for *those* activities. That makes perfect sense, and it clarifies why I have been feeling so confused and frustrated by the conflicting priorities.'

SETTING UP AND RUNNING TEAMS

'Welcome, everyone.' The chairman of the meeting looked around the room. 'And welcome to those of you who have dialled into the meeting by video.'

Everyone looked up at the video screen. One of the video participants appeared to be talking animatedly.

Everyone sang out in unison. 'You are on mute.'

'Sorry. I was saying, am I supposed to be in this meeting? My name was in the invite, but I do not know what it is all about.'

'Of course you do.' replied the chairman. 'You are the technical expert in our Rapid Cost Optimisation (RCO) cross-functional team.'

'Oh, is that what RCO stands for?'

'Yes, didn't you read the email?'

Chris wrote the date on the top of his notepad and started listing the names of everyone to look busy. He had no idea what this meeting was about either.

Things went from bad to worse after that, and after an hour of talking around in circles, they ran out of time and agreed to meet again a week later.

Chris went back to his office and dialled Sonya. He wanted to understand what went wrong.

'Chris, the reason many teams are ineffective is that the team is never formally launched. When this RCO team was formed, did anyone make the team goals crystal clear? Were those goals aligned across the business? Did everyone who was part of the team know what their role was?

'Usually, there needs to be a permanent *core* team who are accountable for team outcomes. The *extended* team members can be brought in, when needed, to help with specific aspects of the project. Also, include any stakeholders who could hinder progress and get their buy-in upfront. In some cases, it may even be helpful to have *external* team members such as suppliers get involved. The point is everyone should know their roles.'

'Well, I certainly didn't know my role,' said Chris.

'Too often, in the interests of getting some actions done quickly, leaders ignore the establishment phase of a team.

'For your functional team, Chris, remember you also need to define clear boundaries. Empowerment fails unless clear boundaries and disciplines are established and communicated at the start.'

'What do you mean by boundaries?'

'Things like spending and decision-making limits. HR policies, reporting deadlines, behavioural and attitude norms.'

'Aha, you are reminding me about my authority as the manager?'

Sonya nodded. Peter Drucker said, 'Every decision that impacts our lives will be made by the person who has the power to make that decision, not the "right" person, or the "smartest" person, or the "best" person.' Chris, remember that influence is very different to authority. Read up about it in the *Leader's Guide.*'

Chris put the phone down, and on the weekend, he read the section on management authority.

MANAGEMENT AUTHORITY

An organisation gives a manager authority to enforce order and structure to meet the minimum requirements of the business. While much of the focus in leadership training and development is on inspirational leadership and personal infiuence, it is ineffective unless built on the foundation of a compliant and well-disciplined team.

Chris finished reading the section and wrote in his notebook:

- *Share the minimum behavioural standards and attitudes expected with my team*
- *Make the team fully aware of their limits of empowerment, including spending limits and decision-making*
- *Explain and enforce the HR policies*
- *Define the limits of flexibility regarding time-keeping and whereabouts*
- *Set and enforce deadlines for reporting and administration*
- *Establish a set of well-understood ground rules with the team on things like meeting disciplines, emails, reports and proactive communication*

Chris sighed. 'So what am I supposed to do? When am I supposed to be an authoritative manager using my authority to get things done, and when do I lead through influence and inspiration?'

At that moment, his youngest son Nathan walked in the door with shoulders hunched and a sour look on his face. 'I don't want to go to the football match today.'

'Why not?'

'I don't enjoy it. The coach keeps making me play as a defender, so I never score any goals. It's not fun.'

Chris firmly placed two hands on his son's shoulders. 'Nat, a defender is one of the most important people on the field. You cannot win matches if the opposing team scores more goals against you than you do against them.

Hey, let's count the number of goals you *save* today. Okay? Remember what we said about finishing something that you started. We have committed to the coach and the other players to play until the end of the season. At that time, you can re-evaluate if you still want to play. Now get your football kit, or we will be late. We will talk about strategies to save goals in the car.'

As Nathan fetched his kit, Chris closed his *Leaders Guide* and decided to forget about management training for the rest of the day.

On his way home, he and Nathan discussed the game.

'So, how did it go?' Chris asked.

'Dad, now that I know my role is to save goals, I counted four goals that absolutely would have been scored if I wasn't there. The coach mentioned my name in our wrap up, and now I feel much better about being on the team.'

Chris smiled down at his son. He enjoyed having Nathan as a captive audience to chat to all the way home.

Before he went to bed, Chris wrote himself an action plan:

Action plan:

1. Write out a high-level job description for each person in the team, including me, making sure there are no gaps or overlaps.
2. Make sure each person on the team knows their role and understands their unique contribution.
3. Define the reporting structure.
4. Define a reporting template and governance structure for internal as well as customer communication.
5. Set up a weekly coffee chat and monthly breakfast session so that the team can get to know each other.
6. Set up a team kick-off workshop to get buy-in on why the team exists and explain the operational governance described above.
7. Clarify team outputs and define customer measures. Document the KPI's.
8. Ensure that each team member also shares what voluntary activities

they are involved in outside this team structure to be factored into their overall work priorities.

Chris made a note to define deadlines for his plan and allocated time in his Outlook calendar to work on it. He needed to lock in dates in his team's calendar so that everyone would be available, including Pierre.

Chris opened his book.

RUNNING TEAMS - THE PDM OPERATIONAL MODEL

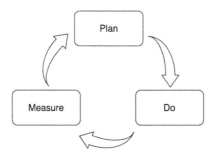

The PDM model (*Plan - Do - Measure*) defines an *operational cycle* that is incredibly powerful when its full impact is understood and practised. The operational model is so important that entire chapters have been devoted to each stage in this cycle, but an overview of the cycle will be explained here:

The cycle starts with **planning**. All team activities should begin with a clear understanding of the reasons that something must be done - *the why.* There is a truism "slow to start, quick to finish." Team leaders often compromise on getting buy-in upfront in the interests of time, only to lose time later on when it is clear that full commitment was not obtained. Without commitment, excuses for failure, and reasons given for why things cannot be done, start to dominate the conversation.

During the planning process, a clear understanding of the *output*, the *customer* (the person that receives the output), and the customer's *measure* of success should be obtained.

The second phase is to **do** what the plans dictated. It will be seen in greater detail later on, that the secret to getting things done is at some point to stop planning and questioning *the why* and get on with completing the actions.

Lastly, outputs should be **measured** to see if the plans have actually produced the expected outcomes. This review of the *measured* results is what then drives the re-planning to restart the cycle.

Chris slammed the book down, grinning. 'I cannot believe how I missed the significance of this model before. Academically I understood the cycle, but I kept thinking, "so what?" I think I am now starting to understand why Taylor was wrong, but also why he was right.'

Chris paged forward in his book to see that the following three chapters of the textbook were dedicated to this model. He had mixed feelings about delving further into the model. He had experienced his 'aha' moment and wanted to move onto a more exciting topic.

WHAT IS A PLAN?

Chris sat down at his favourite coffee shop and waited for Sonya to join him. He opened his book and started reading.

PLANNING

The first phase in the PDM operational cycle for running teams is planning.

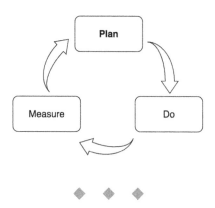

◆ ◆ ◆

Chris stared at the diagram in front of him. 'Sonya must be kidding if she thinks I am going to read an entire chapter on planning. I have seen so many plans come and go, and the plans become out of date before the ink is dry. In the past, it made sense for people to plan, but I think it is better to get on with things and stop wasting time talking about what you plan to do. How many planning meetings have I sat through, and how many plans have I read that ended up being a complete waste of time because things change so fast? I will discuss this with Sonya. Hopefully, I can skip forward to a more interesting topic.'

Sonya arrived, and they placed their usual coffee order. After a while, the owner came over and apologised for the delay in their order. Someone had called in sick at the last minute. Chris smiled sympathetically. He hoped this delay would illustrate his point perfectly to Sonya.

'Sonya, I wanted to ask you if you agree I can skip the planning chapter. I think planning was relevant back in the past when the pace of change was slower. Today things change so fast that plans are a waste of time. Would you not agree that we would have more time to get the job done if we didn't spend so much time planning?'

Chris pointed over to the planning board next to the coffee machine. 'Look at that coffee roster, Sonya.'

Sonya studied the work schedule. Each staff member had their name typed in different colours, during specific time slots over the coming weeks, for easy reference.

'Somebody spent a lot of time planning that schedule.' Chris said. 'And now someone has called in sick, so it is *meaningless*.'

Chris paused for effect and leaned back as though he had moved a chess piece into a checkmate position.

Sonya paused, wishing her coffee had arrived as a distraction to gather her thoughts. Chris *didn't know what he didn't know*. Few things make coaching less effective than trying to help someone who already thinks they have all the answers.

Eventually, Sonya spoke. 'The error in your judgement, Chris, is to confuse *the plan* with the process of planning. We need planning *because* things will change. Can you imagine if there was no schedule, and someone called in sick? Where would you even start when looking for a replacement?'

Sonya pointed to the schedule. 'The main benefit of the so-called *plan* is to adapt to change. The error people make is in wasting time on the planning document itself. It would be far more practical if the planning board were flexible. Imagine if the plan had each barista scheduled on the planning board with sticky notepaper. You could easily move staff around as things change. That professional-looking, colour-coded *plan* is not where the value of planning lies.'

Chris looked sheepish as he reflected on how often he had made the mistake of thinking of the plan in terms of a document, rather than a powerful and effective way of adapting to change in a structured and predetermined way.

Sonya smiled at Chris. 'Now are you ready to read up on planning?'

Chris had one last attempt to get out of reading more about planning. 'Sonya, I agree with everything you have said, but don't you agree that when we have so little free time, it is better to start *doing* things rather than wasting time *planning* what you will do? I'm an action guy, and I actually don't mind being busy. When I am doing something, I feel far more productive than when I am idly thinking or making theoretical plans.'

'Chris, have you ever considered that busyness is a form of laziness? Being busy, to avoid thinking about why you are doing what you are doing misses the point of good management.'

With a somewhat deflated look, Chris nodded sheepishly and tucked the book under his arm as he went back to his office, promising to read it with an open mind.

Later that evening, Chris took out his book and continued reading.

PLANNING IS A PROCESS

Dwight Eisenhower said: "In preparing for battle I have always found that plans are useless, but planning is indispensable."

Retired Army General Stanley McChrystal, in his book *Team of Teams* (2015), brilliantly captures the challenge we face with planning. In it, he contrasts complexity with complication. "Complexity produces a fundamentally different situation from the complicated challenges of the past; complicated problems require great effort but ultimately yielded to prediction. Complexity means that, in spite of our increased abilities to track and measure, the world has become, in many ways, vastly less predictable."

Chris re-read that statement a few times to see if he really understood it. 'I suppose building fighter jet aircraft is *complicated*. There are many moving parts, but a blueprint can be produced of what parts are needed and how to construct it. Describing how to fly the plane into battle is *complex*. There are so many variables that it would be impossible to specify in advance exactly what to do in every situation or every route travelled. In fast-moving, complex environments, detailed plans that dictate each step of execution will fail. The more structured and predictable the environment and circumstances, the more relevant the plan. However, it is the act of planning that prepares us for agile execution of the plan in a dynamic environment.'

Satisfied that he understood the previous paragraph, Chris read on.

PLAN THE JOURNEY

All businesses are set up to achieve something, and all teams are initiated for a specific purpose. Every person is hired to achieve something very specific. It is essential to get the entire team aligned to achieve those goals. Otherwise, any proactiveness from empowered team members could be misguided.

To set aligned goals, start at the end and ask, "*What outcome do we require?*"

Knowledge workers are motivated by achieving something. They don't want just to do a job or task; they want to contribute to something. Skilled staff want to understand the purpose. They want to know what journey they are on.

Planning is about describing the journey details:

- Where are we going?
- Why is it important to get there?
- What route are we taking?
- Who is going?
- What are the milestones?

THE POWER OF A COMMON VISION

Over 50 years ago, President Kennedy urged the American nation to achieve an audacious goal - to land on the moon. "We choose to go to the moon in this decade and do the other things, not because they are easy, but because they are hard." Kennedy understood the power of a common vision.

All teams should have a clear *vision*. A vision statement is important because it is the first step to achieving alignment. If team members are going to display leadership by operating outside of their core job role, it is imperative that they understand the team's overall goal. A good team vision sets the overall direction. It defines why the team exists. A good vision is emotive, and team members can visualise what it *feels* like. When looking forward, team members get a sense of excitement and are energised by it.

A vision is not necessarily realistic. In Jim Collins' excellent book *Good to Great* (2001), he refers to the vision as a Big Hairy Audacious

Goal (BHAG). Teams that have an exciting vision are more energised and motivated to high performance.

The need to achieve a goal is so strong that team members will make up a goal that makes sense to them without a clear vision. The danger of the team making their own goal up is that teams can end up being busy doing activities and going in a direction not understood or supported by the overall business. A good vision keeps the team on track to achieve the overall reason for forming the team.

Strategy defines the unique way that long-term goals will be achieved. *Strategic objectives* define long-term goals that are linked to a specific approach to achieve them. These strategies can be translated into *strategic initiatives, personal objectives,* and ultimately, daily *plans.*

Chris paused. Was Sonya wanting him to create a vision for the team and then define strategic objectives? He had seen these statements in the wider business, and they were so wordy and nebulous that he could not see how they added any value.

'Our vision is to enhance the lives of every person on the planet.' He pretended to gag as he muttered the words.

'Strategy needs to drive specific operational decisions; otherwise, it is meaningless.' Chris thought. *'Achieving growth via acquiring new customers* is a totally different strategy to *achieving growth through selling more to existing customers.* Each approach requires different skillsets and different operational processes.'

Chris thought back to a previous non-strategic manager he had worked for, whose mantra was "a dollar is a dollar." The company would sell anything to anyone so long as it increased sales in the short term. Long term, the business ran at a loss as there was no clarity on what business they were set up to be *operationally.*

Chris studied the diagram in his textbook.

'If I ignore all the airy-fairy words, I need to get the strategic objectives to engage the gears of the strategic initiatives, which in turn drives the daily priorities of the team. I need to get the *doing* phase aligned with the strategic *plans*.'

Chris took out his notepad and wrote out his interpretation of what planning meant to him, to discuss with Sonya the following morning.

Define:

- *The 'why' - the reason the team exists*
- *The key outputs or focus areas of the team*
- *Who the customers are for these outputs (both internal and external)*
- *Key deliverables and customer measures required for each focus area*
- *How the team contributes to the strategic goals of the business*
- *The team's focus and priorities (deciding what really matters)*
- *How the team initiatives link to the company objectives*
- *The required monthly, weekly, daily actions to* achieve the above

Chris looked over the notes he had written with smug satisfaction. 'I will talk to Sonya in the morning about my plans for the kick-off meeting. It is going to be a winner!'

THE INTERFACE CUSTOMER

Chris ushered Sonya into the conference room with eager anticipation. 'I intend to arrange a team kick-off meeting in the office.' Chris said. 'I will invite the core and extended team members, so I get buy-in from all the stakeholders. I have also thought about how I can include Pierre, so he feels part of the team.'

'That's great, Chris. If you want buy-in, you always need to remember, "why before what." Starting with goals helps people understand "the why." Sonya then added to his ideas.

'Ideally, you want to fly Pierre in for the meeting, but I do understand that practically it is not always possible. Video conferencing is a good alternative.'

'Yes, I have arranged the sessions so that Pierre can dial into the sessions most relevant to him, and I have been mindful of the time-zone differences.'

Sonya smiled, mindful of her feedback to Chris from Pierre. 'If practical, I recommend you hold the meeting offsite. When someone goes to a location away from the office, they think differently. You want the team to get out of operational mode and stop focusing on day-to-day problems.

The goal is to think strategically about the overall purpose of the team and what results are required. The office environment is a constant reminder of the present. Also, in the office, team meetings are interrupted.

'Meeting offsite also creates a natural opportunity for team-building, such as sharing lunch together. For those who cannot meet face-to-face, don't forget about them in the breaks. You might have a few social sessions online, where you meet informally with no business agenda.

'Where practical, extend the planning session to include people in other departments who contribute to the team outputs and also include contractors and even suppliers.

'Also, make sure you don't arrive with all the answers. For buy-in, you want to make sure the team can genuinely contribute to the plans.

'Good planning contributes to effective teamwork. A big mistake I see in many organisations is that they measure good teamwork only by great attitudes or going the extra mile. Both traits are ingredients for success but ironically can make things a lot less effective unless the team has defined goals and roles. Take a football team as an example. If everyone rushed onto the field with a great attitude and lots of enthusiasm, the game would be chaotic, and few goals would ever be scored.'

This conjured up an image for Chris of one of Nathan's first football matches when he played for the Under 7's. The boys had been so enthusiastic to kick the ball and score goals that many of them had actually scored goals for the opposing team without even realising it.

Sonya drew Chris back from his thoughts. 'As you know, I recently travelled to Paris. In addition to attending the trade show, I visited this engineering organisation, and they had figured out the roles, but not the *interfaces* we talked about earlier. They would have benefited from that diagram you did for the Grand Prix tyre changing team.'

Sonya sketched out the equivalent diagram for the engineering team.

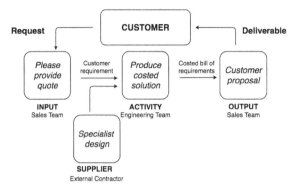

'The team *roles* were clear. What was missing is that each team had no clarity about who their *interface customer* was, for their *output*. Instead of each team working with defined inputs and outputs, they figuratively threw deliverables into the ring as they were completed.

'The culture of this organisation was "above-and-beyond." They aimed to work as a team, but they had no shared plan and no mapping out of roles, responsibilities, and handover points. Everyone was involved, but unique ownership was unclear.

'Engineering produced the bill of materials, but some design work was so specialised that external contracting companies were involved. Salespeople often contacted these specialist contractors directly, bypassing the engineering team, and so premature information was used for indicative pricing to the customer. The engineering team would also bypass the sales team to clarify requirements with the end customer because they felt the sales team had insufficient technical expertise to define the requirements. By the time the final design was done, and the *real* pricing was determined, everyone was unhappy. The team worked hard, had a great attitude, and did "whatever-it-takes" to get the job done, but the end product was far from ideal.

'Here is how it should have worked.

'The *sales team* defines the requirements by talking to the customer.

The sales team should be the only official interface from the customer to the organisation.

'The engineering team is the interface team to the sales team. The input to the *engineering team* is the requirements of the customer communicated through the sales team. There is no issue in the engineering team talking directly to the end customer so long as the official interface and the ownership of that engagement is via the sales team.

'The engineering team design a technical solution and produce a costed solution, and their output is a costed bill of materials.

'The interface customer of the engineering team is the sales team, even though the end customer uses the design. The external contractor is a supplier to the engineering team, and therefore any interaction with sales is owned by the engineering team.

'There is no issue in sales dealing directly with the specialist contractor, so long as the ownership of that engagement remains with engineering. If these interfaces were correctly managed, everyone would have been aligned, and the end customer would have had a better experience.

'Using this operational model ensures that the sales team cannot pass premature information to the end customer until they receive the output from the engineering team. In this way, you avoid the chaos that exists in many multi-dimensional teams.

'An organisation that follows siloed, functional job roles with no commitment to satisfy the end customer is equally unacceptable.

'The middle ground is to create your team plan with clear definitions of handover points and deliverables, and then when people play out of position or go above-and-beyond, they do so within well-defined boundaries, with complete alignment with the rest of the team.

'A key goal of your kick-off meeting is to get this alignment and understanding of outputs, together with the clarity of who the interface customers are that need those outputs.

'Good luck with your kick-off. Please tell me how it goes.'

'I will,' said Chris, and they both departed.

Later on, Chris walked over to the cafe with his notebook and ordered his coffee, extra hot as always.

He paged back in his notes to find the diagram he had produced for the Grand Prix, to see how an interface customer fitted into the model. He recognised the Lollipop man as the interface customer between the driver and the team activities. Chris recalled watching Australian driver Mark Weber's wheel flying off his car as he pulled off from a pitstop in the 2013 German Grand Prix. The Lollipop man had made an error and signalled to the driver to go before confirming the tyre was fastened. 'Management is a big responsibility,' he thought to himself.

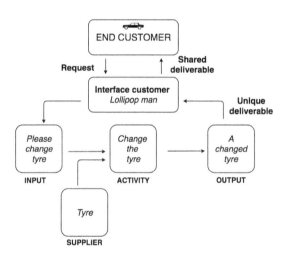

He was busy updating his diagram when his coffee finally arrived, but it was lukewarm. Evidently, it had been made earlier and left to get cold on the countertop.

Chris sent the coffee back. An argument ensued between the barista and the waitress as to whose fault it was. The barista blamed the waitress for not taking it out soon enough, and she blamed him for not alerting her to the fact that it was ready.

Chris applied his model to this interaction and immediately noticed the root cause. Instead of the barista identifying the waitress as his interface customer, he had put his *output*, the coffee, in no-man's-land.

Chris reflected on how many times that mistake was made at work with people sending out an email into the ether with no proper handover to their customer.

Chris left the coffee shop feeling motivated. He was confident about how he planned to proceed with the kick-off.

THE TEAM KICK-OFF

Friday had arrived. Chris's team of twelve people gathered at the Moreton Ridge Conference Centre and got to know each other better over a delicious breakfast. The breakfast table looked over a beautiful lake that almost encircled the centre. The mood was relaxed but professional. After coffee, Chris rounded the group up into the meeting room. An icebreaker soon had the group in howls of laughter. His *head* wondered if he had taken the fun factor too far - his *heart* confirmed that it was going well. People wanted to be there, and communication barriers were breaking down, which would prove useful later when they tackled tough topics. Chris reflected how his desire for efficiency had often stifled creativity and inhibited getting the best out of people.

Chris addressed the group and explained the goals of the day. 'The priority of the day is to establish "the why," Chris said. He went on to explain how he planned to include Pierre. 'Pierre will dial in via video conference to some sessions, and I have also collected his inputs prior to the meeting for sessions he won't attend. I have also arranged a conference walk-about where I will share our surroundings via my phone camera, so he gets a feel for the place.'

Chris talked about how he wanted to establish a common team *vision* statement. He explained why the team was formed and how it was expected to contribute to the overall business goals.

To get the group working together, Chris facilitated a group SWOT analysis. 'The acronym stands for Strengths, Weaknesses, Opportunities and Threats.'

Strengths	Weaknesses
Opportunities	Threats

While keeping the SWOT in mind, they then defined the Critical Success Factors (CSF). 'CSFs are the critical things that need to be done to achieve the team goals.' Chris said.

Having summarised a condensed list of items, the team then documented the Enablers and Inhibitors. '*Enablers,*' Chris said, 'are things needed to achieve those goals, while *inhibitors* are things that will stop the team from achieving it.'

Chris explained the process they were going through was what he called *gap management*. 'Gap management requires analysis of where the team is now, and where the team wants to be at a specific future date, to devise a plan to close the gap.'

Key questions he put to the group were:

+ What things are really key?
+ What does success look like?
+ What does failure look like?

After establishing the team vision, Chris helped the team define their **team objectives**. Some team members were sceptical, as they had seen this approach fail on many past occasions.

Chris addressed the group. 'Many companies have introduced some form of Managing by Objectives (MBO's) in the last few decades, but the process has failed because of poor execution. Properly applied, working to set objectives can be the most powerful tool to achieving proactive progress.'

He talked about how Google and other successful companies had successfully applied OKR's (Objectives and Key Results). 'Businesses that have no long-term objectives become focused on *reacting* to problems rather than proactively addressing the causes of the problems or innovating to create new opportunities.'

Chris wanted to illustrate the process. 'My daughter Evelyn plays tennis. Every Saturday morning, we take her to the local tennis courts for coaching. They have a ball machine that fires tennis balls across the court in a pseudo-random way. It shoots the balls in a way that she cannot predict, but it is programmed to allow her to focus on a specific return shot. This process is improving her ball hitting skills. Now imagine if the machine was faulty and started shooting balls in all directions. The OKR would be to fix the machine, not to collect the stray balls more quickly and efficiently. Your time would also be better spent working on the OKR rather than telling other people how badly the machine is performing or whose fault it is that it is not working.

'The ball machine represents the systems and processes that have been developed in the past for us to deliver our solutions to our customers. Nobody understands how well that is working or what deficiencies there are better than us. Consider these objectives as mini projects that improve the machinery. It is imperative for us to understand the machine. A machine takes inputs, processes them, and delivers outputs.

'The first thing for us to ask is, "who wants the outputs we deliver?" This defines our *customer,* and our customer cares about our outputs, not our activities. Once we have defined the objective, we need to measure the improvements with the yardstick of our customer.'

Chris then shared with the team what he had learnt about setting SMARTS objectives. 'The acronym stands for Specific, Measurable, Achievable, Realistic, Time-bound and Stretching. The most crucial aspect is to set specific, measurable objectives to be achieved within a stated timescale. Instead of "keep customers happy", replace it with "improve our Net Promoter Score (NPS) by 10% by the end of the financial year." By the way, the S was added to SMART to get a stretch component into the objectives to balance out the realistic and achievable aspect.'

Chris shared some of Sonya's real-world observations about setting objectives with the team.

- Keep objectives simple and do not have too many
- Use day-to-day English, and not 'management speak'
- Get buy-in from all the stakeholders
- Build in flexibility to achieve the spirit of the objective
- Set interim milestones and monitor regularly
- Chunk long-term goals into bite-sized activities that get integrated into the day-to-day priorities

'We must all share a common goal, and it is also important that each of us knows what our unique contribution is to achieve those goals. Remember the other day when we did not have clarity about who was updating the project plan and who was contacting the customer? I confess my role is to help you with that. I apologise. I shunned my responsibility as team leader. Let's go over that example again and define exactly who is uniquely responsible for each aspect of the customer deliverable so that there are no overlaps and no gaps.'

The team finished analysing the situation. Chris wrapped up with an encouraging speech, and the team headed for the bar. Chris had arranged for a pool competition between two randomly assigned teams, and he planned to issue forfeits to people who broke a rather complicated set of rules he had developed the night before. Chris was enthusiastically explaining the rules, as well as the associated fun forfeits he had invented when his boss called to find out how the day had gone. He turned to the group. 'Get started without me. I've written it up in a document. You are going to love it.' And with that, he walked out of the room to get some privacy.

With no real idea of what to do and without being convinced that this would actually be *fun*, the group disintegrated, with some bold team members leading the way to order drinks at the bar. By the time Chris rejoined the group, he realised the team had missed the opportunity to engage in his team building exercise, but the team were actually bonding rather well and were discussing the work topics of the day. It was the last day of the working week, and so Chris relaxed a bit and enjoyed a bit of social time with the team. He looked around at this group of people united in purpose and felt that the *kick-off* had gone well.

Chris felt his phone go off in his pocket and looked annoyed at the interruption. He had assumed it was his boss calling again, and he was in no mood to continue talking about work. Instead, it was his wife, and his look of irritation turned to concern. 'Is everything alright, Gwen?'

'No, sorry, I've been called into work. Please come home as soon as possible.'

Chris finished his call and said, 'The best laid plans of mice and men,' misquoting an old Robert Burns poem. With that, he waved his colleague's goodnight and rushed home.

THE EXECUTION PHASE

Championship day! Sonya woke up early on Saturday morning excited to prove her skills after weeks of practise at the driving range. Professional coaching had improved her game. Sonya was a natural at most sports. She had taken to golf like a duck to water and could hit the ball straighter and harder than most women half her age.

Her golf teacher had given her insights into why her handicap was not improving, despite improvements in her game. 'You are too impulsive in the moment. You take unnecessarily risky shots in critical moments on the course, and that is ruining your otherwise impressive scorecard.' Together, they worked out a strategy of how to *crack* the course, and today she vowed to follow her game plan.

Everything was going well until the 13th hole. The 13th hole was notorious for people ruining their scorecard. Her game plan was to hit a conservative first shot, using her 5-iron to keep herself far away from the trees and bunkers, which complicated this hole.

Sonya was having such a good round that in-the-moment she picked out her chunky driver instead. Sonya figured that a perfect shot off the tee could place the ball beyond any trouble. 'If I hit my drive the same as the previous hole, I could finish this hole in one under par.'

Sonya grimaced as she sliced the ball straight into the trees.

Her game went from bad to worse after that, and when she arrived home, she chastised herself for once again not following her game plan that she meticulously planned the night before. 'Why do I keep making the same mistake week after week after week?' she groaned as she packed her clubs away, waving goodbye to yet another chance to shine in the club championships.

On Monday morning, Chris met with Sonya in the office and before getting into the meat of their coaching session, he listened sympathetically to Sonya's golf woes.

They discussed how easy it was to deviate from your self-made plans. Chris then gave Sonya an update on Friday's kick-off meeting.

The meeting had gone very well. Everyone left feeling motivated. They had aligned goals and documented milestones for their plans. Chris also confessed how his pool game activity at the workshop had failed because he had not followed his recently learnt mantra of "*why* before *what*."

Sonya was encouraged and was keen to link her leadership lessons to Chris's kick-off meeting. She thumbed through Chris's *Leaders Guide* and pointed to the operational Plan-Do-Measure cycle diagram.

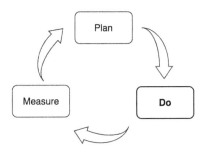

'Chris, the kick-off meeting addresses the Plan and Measure phase of the operational cycle. A key element in the operational cycle is also the DO phase. Leonardo da Vinci said, "I have been impressed with the urgency of doing. Knowing is not enough; we must apply. Being willing is not enough; we must do."

'Chris, we have talked about the fact that teamwork does not imply that the actual work itself is done as group work. In many teams, the members of that team are scattered across multiple geographies or even multiple time zones. The good work that you establish in the Planning phase allows team members to do the work in isolation and yet still be aligned. You have a great set of milestone plans; now the challenge is to *do* what you planned.'

Chris nodded unconvincingly. 'These plans are far from perfect. I've realised that one day probably wasn't enough to plan this properly, but I can't afford to run another session. It took ages to find a day that everyone was available, and it is too expensive to arrange another offsite meeting. I have made a few notes of things I want to change and improve. I'll work on this tonight and send my proposed changes to the team by tomorrow morning.'

Chris was expecting Sonya to compliment him on his high standards and good work ethic and waited patiently for her to respond. Eventually, she spoke.

'Chris, be careful not to confuse planning with procrastination - they look the same. Many teams have great plans and good intentions, yet when it comes down to execution, they go back into planning mode and re-plan instead of doing what they planned to do. Worse still, these new plans are created in isolation, losing all the buy-in created by the collaboration of the original plans. You told me before that you are an action guy. Well, once you have a set of aligned plans, however imperfect, it is time to stop thinking and start doing. Voltaire said, "Perfect is the enemy of good."

'Management guru, the late *Peter Drucker* said, "Plans are only good intentions unless they immediately degenerate into hard work." With that, Sonya waved Chris goodbye and encouraged him to let the team execute the plans that they had already agreed to.

Later that week, Chris followed up to see how everyone was progressing. He was surprised and also disappointed that not a single person was engaged in what they had all agreed were the most important priorities. Somewhat disheartened, he returned to his desk and called Sonya.

'Sonya, you know we talked about the problem of re-planning before going through the Do phase? My problem is not that they are re-planning. My problem is that everyone is busy *doing* something else. When I challenged them about it, in each case they convinced me that what they were distracted with was very important and also urgent. I have the authority to stop them from doing those things, but I am worried about the short-term impact if I do. What do I do now?'

'Chris, the hardest part about executing our plans is starting. Once started, momentum kicks in, and keeping-going is easier. Starting what you agreed at the kick-off is hard, especially if you have not yet chunked it down into actionable activities that can be done in a reasonably short timescale.

'Imagine that you decided to go for an early morning run. Unless you have a clear starting strategy, it is very likely you will procrastinate. Mel Robbins, author of *The 5 Second Rule,* calls it her NASA strategy. When your alarm clock goes off, you count backwards like a rocket launch and then get up before your brain has time to kick in and talk you out of it.

'People's energy is created by the gap between the effort it takes to achieve a desired goal and the benefit of the goal. The trick is to get the gap right. Your team responded to the current apparent crises because they believed their intervention would make an immediate difference, and it was easier to do. The alternative activity, which was predetermined at the kick-off to be *more important,* probably seems too hard for the expected reward, and so they postpone doing it. The task will seem less daunting if it is broken down into bite-sized activities that can be completed in a short period.

'This is why daily and weekly planning is so essential. To get people to work on long-term goals, you need to get your team to define the *next most important activity* linked to the long-term goal and make it a top priority.'

Chris shook his head. 'I don't think it's about priority setting. I think I need to send my whole team, including me, on a time management course. We need more time.'

'Time management is a misnomer,' Sonya said. 'We cannot manage or control time. We are all given exactly the same amount of hours in the day. The real challenge is to manage our *priorities*. Whenever you choose to do one thing, everything else becomes a victim of your choice. It is all about picking the right victims.

'We often prioritise things that are right in front of us or easy to do. We get the short-term reward of responding to a crisis or ticking things off our list, but it's often at the expense of something, or someone, far more important.'

Before Sonya ended the call, she mentioned to Chris there was a chapter about "Time management" in the textbook.

That evening Chris settled down to read.

CAN WE REALLY MANAGE TIME

THE FALLACY OF TIME MANAGEMENT

Time management is not about managing time. Instead, time management is about prioritising important activities in preassigned time slots within our 24 hour day. A helpful process to determine and execute our priorities is *Triage, Decide, Do*.

> Triage > Decide > Do >

TRIAGE

The first step is to Triage all the inputs. In a hospital waiting room, a triage nurse assesses *all* the cases before they can decide which patient is the most urgent and important. It is impossible to know which is the top priority until assessing all the cases. Learning this lesson is key to being more effective in time management.

Triage is about listing all the things we *could* do and then prioritising the most important and urgent things. When we feel stressed about lack of time, we usually have too many things on our mind with no clear idea of when we will address them. The trick is to get everything off our mind and onto a list. This list is not a To-Do list; it may be considered a Could-Do list. Inputs include incoming correspondence, emails, messages, meeting requests, long-term plans and objectives and personal tasks.

The key value of triage is to allow something to be prioritised on its relative rather than absolute merits. In the hospital waiting room, everyone would consider their situation important and urgent. Otherwise, they wouldn't be there. Making something a lesser priority does not mean it is not important. The key insight is that some things are less important or less urgent relative to other things that are higher up the list.

Chris paused. 'Aha. So if I can get the kick-off projects we agreed on chunked into daily bite-sized activities that on a *relative scale* are more important than the daily crises, I will make progress.'

Chris continued reading.

DECIDE

After triage, the next step is to **decide**.

- **Decide "if"** – To paraphrase Yoda from Star Wars, "*There is no such thing as try. There is "do" or "do not do."* Our to-do lists become unmanageable and unachievable when they are full of things that we will *try* to do.
- **Decide "what"** – Once an activity has been prioritised as something that *must be done*, the "what" should be defined. The full scope and quality of the "what" can only be determined when linked to the available time to complete it.

- **Decide "when"** - What time slot is actually available to do the work? Failure to identify a free time slot would be like rushing a patient through to an empty doctors' room because we hadn't first checked if the doctor was actually available. Also, recognise that the value of time is not linear. Although our time system creates neat, equal divisions of time as the earth rotates around the sun, our bodies do not conform to this uniformity. Each of us has some parts of the day where we are far more effective, mentally and physically than others. Do the most important and mentally demanding tasks during these peak-energy times.
- **Decide "who"** - Managers who are pressed for time and want the job done to their own high standards often feel it's just easier to do everything themselves. While that may be initially true, the problem is that the team members never learn, and so the manager becomes overworked. Delegation is a critical skill to be an effective manager.

DO

The final step is to do what was planned to do. Develop a reputation for getting important things done. Set time aside to work on the true priorities of the business in a planned and uninterrupted way. Chunk the non-urgent but important work into bite-sized executable daily tasks that can be prioritised and 100% completed in the allocated time slot. Chunking is the secret to making progress on long-term objectives in an environment of daily operational demands and distractions. Chunking highlights the urgency of important tasks.

Chris stopped reading. Distractions were his number one thing that ate into his available time, and he wanted to know how to stay focused.

He felt it was all very well and good having well-defined priorities, but no one else in the organisation ever respected that.

Chris discussed his dilemma with Sonya in his coaching session the following Thursday.

'Chris, handling every crisis and responding positively to every demand on your time can often be a distraction to true progress. A genuine crisis is something that needs immediate attention to avoid a serious business consequence. Many things that are urgently requested are not as important as the task that they interrupt. The urgency required to make progress on the most important things can often be overlooked by the urgency of the less important thing. Impatience can thus drive many unimportant things to become prioritised. Isn't it interesting how life goes on when we are not around, and yet when we are physically present, we are told the world will stop if we don't drop everything we are doing to handle the current crisis?

'A useful way to assess if something is a crisis or not is to ask: "If this is *not* dealt with right now, what is the consequence to the business?" The second question to ask is, "If this *is* dealt with right now, what is the consequence to the business?" This second question focuses our attention on the risk of delaying the activity that was previously considered to be the *most important* and *most urgent* thing to do.

'In our "always-available" business culture, many managers do not always appreciate that even something as well-meaning as answering the phone changes their priorities. Whatever they had previously planned to do is now less of a priority than this call. The same is true if someone interrupts a meeting or changes the topic.

'Many businesses live in a perpetual crisis cycle. Let's use a fire analogy. In the workplace, immediate fires crop up all the time. A customer has a complaint. A design is not working to specification. Equipment is delayed from a supplier. A staff member calls in sick. Your presence is required at a project review. The list goes on and on. Good fire management requires the fire department to burn a strip of land under controlled conditions, to strip the land of fuel, thus acting as a firebreak. Usually, longer-term plans are the equivalent of preparing a fire break. Managers find it incredibly hard to let fires burn while they are preparing a fire break, yet, with the odd exception, this is exactly what is required.'

'Great, Sonya, good insights, but I still don't understand how I can tell the person with the current fire that I am going to ignore them to head off for my fire break activity.'

'Chris, firstly *share* your fire break priority with the other person. See if you can park the current issue or delay addressing it to a set time after dealing with your true top priorities. I am not saying it is easy. I am saying that if you always prioritise the current urgent fire, you will never get ahead of the fire to protect more important assets. Very often addressing today's crisis actually *causes* tomorrow's crisis, hence the vicious crisis cycle that is created.'

'Oh, how true that is around here.' Chris said. 'For example, today I had an escalation asking me to deal directly with a customer unhappy with our speed of response. To get the background information before I called them, I had to spend an hour getting a detailed briefing of all the customer issues, as well as where our internal processes had slowed us down in responding. The irony of this story is that it turned out the root cause was the very process I was busy trying to fix when I became distracted by this customer issue. The underlying cause is affecting far bigger clients than this one, and by me not making progress on the solution, all our customers are continuing to be negatively affected. I suppose the lesson I am learning is that it is sometimes acceptable to ignore a current issue, so long as it addresses something even more important.'

THE FALLACY OF
MULTI-TASKING

It was the weekend. Chris was trying to read his *Leaders Guide* book, but his kids were trying to get his attention to watch them play a computer game.

'Did you see that, Dad?' Liam asked.

Chris had half-heartedly been trying to follow the game while also reading his book. 'Of course I did, buddy. Great move.' Chris did not look up from his book.

Liam shrugged his shoulders with a disappointed look and a knowing glance across to his siblings and continued playing.

Using his peripheral vision, Chris watched Liam re-engage in his game as he continued reading. He felt proud of how he was able to balance work and family demands.

MULTI-TASKING

Multi-tasking should be avoided, but multiple-tasking is one of the first skills a new manager needs to develop. As a technical expert, it is often not possible to move onto a new task or project until the current one is finished. As a manager, there are usually a number of major activities that all have to be done in parallel. Inexperienced managers can end up literally trying to do more than one task at a time. Instead of chunking their major tasks into serial chunks that allow progress on multiple tasks, they fool themselves into thinking they can work on many of them at the same time.

Over 2000 years ago, the Latin writer Publilius Syrus said, "To do two things at once is to do neither."

Today, neuroscience is helping to prove that he was right. Our Pre-Frontal Cortex (PFC), the part of our brain where intelligent, rational thinking takes place, is a serial processor. Unlike the rest of our brain, it cannot do two things simultaneously and only creates the illusion of multi-tasking by switching quickly between tasks. Scientists tell us that this switching process actually reduces our cognitive performance on each task. While creating the illusion of efficiency, this ineffective process of multi-tasking is actually having a very negative effect on the workplace. Managers end up being frantically busy working on multiple priorities yet finishing none.

There is even a name for this process of mental channel switching. Massachusetts psychiatrist, Edward Hallowell, in his book *CrazyBusy*, calls it "Frazzing - frantic ineffective multi-tasking." Frazzing reduces productivity as, when interrupted, the first thing we say when we get back to the original task is, "now, *where was I?*" as we reload all the lost data back into our short-term memory for processing. Often the time taken to execute the task is less than the mental setup time, which is lost through interruptions.

In 2010, Christopher Chabris and Daniel Simons published a book called *The Invisible Gorilla*, which goes a long way to proving our inability to multi-task. The book title is a reference to an experiment where a man in a gorilla suit literally walks into the midst of a group of people. Because they are focused on something else, they don't see the gorilla. Of course, they do *see it* with their eyes, but they are not consciously aware of seeing it, as their mental attention is somewhere else. This is called *inattention blindness.*

Chris reflected on a recent near accident he had experienced while driving to work. He had been talking on his car phone and trying to solve a rather complex issue that they were having in the engineering lab. His mind was far away when he suddenly noticed that the traffic had come to a standstill from an accident, and he had narrowly avoided crashing into the back of the stationary truck in front of him. As his awareness became attuned to his environment, he was shocked that he had not noticed the accident, the line of stationary cars, or the massive truck in front of him. He recalled asking himself, 'how could I have been so blind?'

Chris put his book down and looked around the room. He immediately became aware that although he was with his kids physically, mentally he had been somewhere else. He crawled onto the floor and grabbed the games controller playfully. 'Right, now I'll show you who is the king of this game.'

His children's faces lit up as Chris really engaged in their game for the first time that evening.

The following morning Chris took out his trusty notebook and made some more notes.

Time-management steps:

- *Triage everything that could be done*
- *Decide what must be done*
- *Decide what to delegate*
- *Prioritise the "most urgent, most important" items*
- *Chunk the task to fit an available time slot*
- *Schedule the task in your calendar*
- *Make sure you finish the chunked task*

DELEGATION

Back in the office on Monday, Chris made his way down the corridor to a vacant meeting room, where he was meeting Sonya.

'Hi Chris, what is top of mind for you today?'

'I have realised if I am to stop trying to multi-task, I need to pass more things down to the team to do. Any advice on delegation from your years of experience leading teams?'

'Sure. Firstly, remember that when you delegate downwards, you still own the issue upwards. Good delegation starts with clarity about what you are delegating. Usually, it is better to delegate an entire project, or section of a project, because there is a sense of responsibility for the outcome, not just the tasks. People are motivated and perform better if they do fulfilling work and know why the work is important. Also, provide a clear scope of what is being delegated, what the timescales are, how success will be measured and how progress will be reviewed.

'When delegating, make sure the other person is clear what the deliverable is. To be sure that they truly understand what you expect, ask them to describe what *done* looks like.'

'What would you say is the competence mix of the people in your team?'

'Well, Fred and Madison are experienced veterans. Emily and Rodrigues are new recruits, and Joshua and Pierre have been here for at least a couple of years. Why is that relevant?'

'When delegating to competent, experienced people, it is more important to review the results, than how they have been obtained. For people who are new or inexperienced, you may want to be more directive and look at how they achieved the results, but also remember that when you do that, *your method* may be blamed for not achieving results.

'When delegating, support and training may also be needed. Make sure when you delegate the task that you also delegate your authority. Communicate to other key staff and management that you have delegated some of your authority. You want your team members to get the same operational support that you would get.

'Delegation requires a level of trust. Remember when we first met, I wanted to address the issue of trust with you.

'Trust is the first step to building a team. Without first forming trusting relationships, there is nothing to build on.

'There are two elements of trust. Firstly, trust in *intentions*. Do I trust their character and integrity? Secondly, trust in *ability*. Has the person demonstrated they have competence in this specific task?

'Trust in intentions, especially with technical people, is strongly linked to respect. Technical people have personal pride in their expertise, and when managers are dismissive of their contributions or demeaning about their status, they feel disrespected. This creates mistrust that management does not have their best interest at heart and damages the relationship, leading to withholding respect by the technical expert. The lack of mutual respect has a downward spiral effect, as once management perceives that the technical experts are not respecting them, they often act in ways that reinforce the perception of a lack of respect. Often managers link the lack of trust and disrespect from technical people to their own lack of technical expertise rather than the lack of recognition of the status and contribution of technical experts.

'Trust in *ability* is a separate thing to trust in *intentions*. When a close friend gives you medical advice, you may have no doubt that they have good intentions and that they are trustworthy. Still, you would be better off trusting your doctor for a diagnosis of your symptoms, as your friend may have no demonstrable competence in this area.

'Be careful with trust, Chris. Trusting your team does not mean you must have blind trust in their abilities. Trust is earned. The chicken-and-egg conundrum is that people cannot demonstrate their abilities and good intentions unless your relationship starts with an inherent level of trust.

'Trust is built up in stages through incremental levels of empowerment. The *do* phase is not just about *completing* tasks that have to be done. It is also about completing those tasks *competently to* achieve, or exceed the required and desired outcome, as defined by the predetermined success measure.

'David Marquet's book *Turn the Ship Around*, talks about empowerment requiring three things: Control, Competency, and Clarity. Team members need to be given some control (authority) to demonstrate appropriate competency and clarity. These three criteria need to function properly as a triangle to allow full empowerment, and there needs to be trust by the leader to hand over control incrementally so that competence can be demonstrated.'

Chris thanked Sonya, and the following day got his team together again.

'Hi everyone. I know you are all busy. I also know that if you are all not busy with the right things, I'm not going to get what I need as the leader of this team. I wanted to share a few thoughts following our recent kick-off meeting.

'How many people have started with the initiatives that we agreed to do at the kick-off?' Chris asked. Most team members looked at the floor, avoiding his gaze.

Madison spoke up. 'Chris, I think we are still 100% committed to doing those things. It is impossible with everything we have on the go at the moment to make progress. I think once this project deadline is over on Friday, we will all have time to start next week.'

Chris smiled supportively, and the team looked relieved that he was not angry. 'Thinking you will have more time in future is one of human nature's biggest delusions. I have been working on that assumption for my entire working life, and it has never been true. As soon as next week arrives, it is as chaotic as this week, and I delude myself into thinking the following week will be different, and it never is. I will ask everyone to commit to locking in 3 hours a week to make progress on our initiatives. I don't mind if you do it in one 3 hour block or whether you break it up into 6 half-hour slots, but that time needs to become sacrosanct for this initiative. Next week, I will ask each one of you to report back on what you have achieved in that chunk of time. Is that a deal?'

The team members realised that Chris was not giving them an option to opt out and so committed to doing it. Chris's phone beeped. He looked down, and a reminder had popped up on his phone calendar that the next 30 minutes were dedicated to working on the business case to upgrade the project scheduling software. Chris had recognised that many hours of his team's time was being wasted using the current archaic software and had committed to his management to provide a business case to upgrade it by the end of the month. Chris closed the meeting and headed back to his cubicle.

Joshua, one of the more experienced members of the team, who had worked with Chris for over a year in his previous role, followed him. Joshua was a solid performer but had a reputation for not getting to the point.

'Chris, have you got a minute?'

Chris opened his phone calendar. 'I'm free at 2pm.'

Joshua looked disappointed that Chris wasn't dropping everything, as he usually did, to be instantly available for any issues that arose, no matter how trivial.

'Is this something that absolutely cannot wait till then?' Chris asked.

'It can wait, but it won't take very long.'

Chris was aware that with Joshua unless time was limited, it always took a long time. He smiled at Joshua. 'I'll be happy to discuss it at 2pm. My top priority at the moment is to make progress on this business plan to get new project scheduling software for everyone.'

Joshua hesitated. 'Alright, thanks, see you at 2pm.' With that, Chris continued on his way, feeling pleased that for once, he was off to do something that could actually move the needle on the measures he had put in place.

MEASURE WHAT MATTERS

Chris stared at the pile of monthly reports on his desk. Sonya had told him to insist on a monthly report from every team member as a means of measuring their results. He leafed through page after page of problems and cries for more resources. 'These reports are not measuring results. They are using the reports to transfer ownership and avoid accountability.'

Chris knew he would struggle to read through all these reports, let alone do anything about solving any of the issues. Chris considered the root cause. 'The team is reporting on problems that have happened in the past. The reports summarise all the *activity* that has already happened and do not address the fundamental issue of measuring the gap between the plans and the actual results. If I am not careful, I could end up getting drawn into a negative spiral by requesting *more* data, *more* analysis and *more* reports that focus on what went wrong and who is to blame.'

Chris reflected on what he had learnt about the PDM operational cycle.

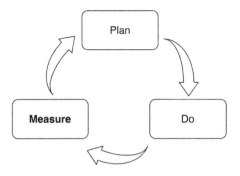

Measuring results comes at the end of the PDM operational cycle, but Chris now realised that the measurement *targets* had to be set during the Planning phase. Because he had not set targets, the reports were collated information and not business management reports. There were no insights of what to improve or lessons learnt to incorporate into the re-planning phase. Chris realised that he would have to be prescriptive about the format of the reports he wanted.

Chris walked over to the coffee shop where he had agreed to meet Sonya. After some social banter, Chris shared his insights about the reports.

Sonya responded. 'Two truisms I believe in are, "you get what you measure" and "people do what is inspected, not expected." Setting measures can be both a blessing and a curse. If you get the measures right, people do the right things to get the right results. If you get the measures wrong, people often knowingly do the wrong things just to comply with the set measures. This is why *setting the right* measures and targets is so essential.

'You have possibly heard that Dr Peter Drucker said, "If you can't measure it, you can't manage it." According to the Drucker Institute, this is not true. Drucker was certainly a big advocate of measurements and actually said, "Work implies...accountability, a deadline and, finally, the measurement of results."

"If you can't measure it, you can't manage it," is misquoted from Dr Edward Deming, who actually said, "It is wrong to suppose that if you can't measure it, you can't manage it." Deming called it "a costly myth."

'Albert Einstein apparently quoted William Bruce Cameron. "Not everything that can be counted counts, and not everything that counts can be counted." Wise words indeed.

'It is important to measure the things that matter, and it is also important to accept that *some* very important measures cannot be quantified with simplistic numerical metrics.

'Measurements help define how well the plans and associated activities are actually working out. They also have a positive benefit of showing the team members how well or badly things are going on the journey. The measure phase provides a feedback mechanism that helps identify cause-effect.'

As Sonya departed, she said, 'Chris, I suggest you read up on Setting Metrics and Targets before our next session on Thursday.'

Chris waved her goodbye and was still deep in thought when he noticed the owner of the coffee shop having a rather heated discussion with his staff. As Chris discretely eavesdropped, he realised the owner was upset because the *maximum* staff-per-day limits had been exceeded on three or four occasions that month.

The duty manager was passionately explaining that he had taken the initiative to ensure that the wait times were minimised.

'But that is my point.' said the owner. 'We agreed to measure the effect of wait times on customer satisfaction with our current staffing levels. If you keep changing the staffing levels, we cannot measure the balance between profitability and customer satisfaction. I have no issue if on an exceptional day you changed the rules, but this has happened multiple times, so now our measures are meaningless.'

As the arguments went back and forth, Chris identified so well with the underlying issue. He had often seen efforts to test his strategy fail when team members made decisions that ignored the measurement systems.

That week he read the section on metrics and measures in preparation for his follow-up meeting with Sonya.

METRICS

Metrics are the quantitative and sometimes qualitative value of something that has been measured. The ultimate measure of customer success is output-based and not *activity-based*. For example, while it may be important for a chef in a restaurant to monitor how beautifully the vegetables are prepared and subsequently displayed on the plate, the ultimate success measure is whether the customer would recommend, and return to, the restaurant.

Activity-based metrics are often easier to define as they are based on clear, objective factors. For example, one could set a target for the engineering team to provide costed designs within 48 hours. While this is easy to measure, the *real* measure of customer satisfaction from the sales team is more complex and subjective. Sometimes, they may want an answer in 8 hours, whereas a week may be a reasonable turnaround in other designs. It may be better to discuss and agree on a target per project, with the metric being the percentage of the design completed within the agreed turnaround time.

A better metric may be for the sales and engineering team to agree, for each design, what the turnaround needs to be, and then track how well the engineering team meets *those* targets. While this may be harder to measure, it is also more meaningful. The point of measures is not to meet them for the sake of meeting them, but to produce a better outcome.

Metrics provide proof of a goal achieved, so it is essential to be able to *actually* measure them. In practice, it is often not trivial and might take weeks or even months to establish the practices and processes to establish the measurement.

There are two types of metrics:

- *Lag metrics* - These are based on measuring what has already happened. Examples are financial metrics such as profit or revenue.

- *Lead metrics* - These are based on measures that are indicators of predicted success. The assumption is the activity will change the result, and therefore, it is essential that the lead indicators genuinely do that. For example, orders booked are a good lead measurement of expected revenue.

Chris finished the chapter and wrote a summary:

- *Measure* trends *to assess longer-term root causes*
- *Measures must be repeatable and reliable*
- *Measures should be objective and relevant*
- *Only measure what matters - ask myself,* "what will I do with these measures?"
- *Don't have too many*
- *Develop a simple dashboard*

Chris reflected on how he could avoid the reports being used to analyse the past, assign blame, or justify why things didn't turn out the way they were planned. He wanted the reports to be used as a scoreboard. *Activity* leads to measured results, but the scoreboard reflects the results, not the activity. Everyone needs to know the score, together with lead measure statistics that show that the activity is achieving the planned outcomes.

Reviewing the measurement data is a key part of the measurement phase, so Chris made notes on how he would define and agree on how the team was going to collaborate, report and communicate:

- *Which meetings must be face-to-face?*
- *Which ones can be by video or phone conference?*
- *What information can be drawn directly from real-time web-based collaboration tools and systems?*
- *What information needs to be disseminated in written reports?*
- *How often should I schedule regular meetings and reports?*

HELP! THEY MADE ME THE MANAGER

Chris also committed to creating an online bulletin board to share all the metrics and management reports. To empower his teams, he needed them to have access to timely, rich, and aligned information.

His daughter Evelyn was sitting at the piano in tears. She was still making mistakes despite diligently practising for months for the upcoming piano recital.

Chris's heart went out to her. Evelyn was so diligent and so unlike Liam. The previous week they had a music festival at the school, and Liam had a solo piece to play on the guitar. He had not practised at all, but he was pretty pleased with his performance and didn't care that he had made a dozen mistakes. Evelyn wanted to play flawlessly and would ruminate for weeks about the most minor error that only a well-trained ear would have heard.

Chris took out his phone and thumbed through his videos on his phone. He played a recording he had made of her playing a year previously.

'Compared to how I sound now, I sounded awful,' she remarked. Then she paused. 'But you know what, Dad, that doesn't actually sound as bad as I remember it.'

'Evelyn, your playing sounds bad to you because you know how you want it to sound. Your audience only hears how it actually sounds. I am going to tape you playing every week. Play that song again, mistakes and all, and we will use it as a *measure* of your current performance. Each week we can refer to your previous recording, and then you can see what progress you are making. Trust me, you sound a lot better than you think you do.'

As Chris recorded the intense little face of his 13-year-old daughter playing the piano so beautifully, his mind drifted to his work situation and the lessons he was learning about operational measures.

'Make a plan and work out how you are going to measure your results. Execute the plan, compare your results against your measures, then adapt the plan. So simple in theory, so hard in practice.'

MEETINGS AND REVIEWING

Sonya read Chris's notes on reviewing his measures.

'Great summary Chris. Remember how I was sharing my frustrations with my golf game? In the club championships, I developed a game plan with a clear head while considering my longer-term goals, but instead of following it, in-the-moment I impulsively re-planned it and then messed it all up.

'While I was playing, I did not have the rich perspective and sense of objectivity that I had the night before. Being adaptable is important, but equally, sticking to your game plan is important.

'This weekend, I was much better at switching off my *planning-head* while I was playing. I adapted my game plan for variables like the wind, but I stuck to my overall strategy. I achieved one over par on that notorious 13th hole, so there were no heroics, but I actually beat my handicap over the full 18 holes. Each time I hit the ball, I only thought about that specific shot and didn't allow myself to plan the next shot until that shot was over. Staying in the *present* helped my game.

'The point of defining the operational Plan-Do-Measure cycle is to separate *planning* from *doing* and also to ensure that the link between the two is the *measure* of success.

'In golf, the operational cycle is set by the course planner. In your team, you will need to set a timescale for each cycle. Within each cycle is a DO phase, and the trick is to ensure that what people actually do is linked to long-term business results, which are part of a mega-cycle.

'Let me explain. Many businesses will set long-term goals that will only culminate in a measure over many years. Within that mega-cycle, there may be sub-cycles such as an annual business plan broken down in quarterly reviews. Those quarterly goals and measures may then be reviewed in a monthly cycle with weekly milestones and within that week to define daily bite-sized results.

'Remember how we said that daily time management was about priority setting and that to achieve a big goal, you need to break it down into small achievable daily chunks of work. How do we eat an elephant? One bite at a time.

'*Agile* has a useful approach where they define each planning loop as a *Sprint*. Outputs are reviewed daily in *a Daily Standup*, where people remain standing to keep the meeting short. Each team member provides feedback on:

- What I finished yesterday
- What I plan to finish today
- Any issues or concerns

'All these activities that they commit to finishing each day link to a masterplan, which is planned in detail for the current *Sprint* cycle (typically a month) but only defined as a high-level milestone after that. This approach works well where you are not 100% sure what the next steps may be, such as when you are innovating and learning along the way, or where you are in a complex, dynamic environment.'

'Sonya, that sounds like a great idea. I'll call a daily meeting for 15 minutes maximum and get everyone to share what they finished yesterday and what they're planning to finish today. It's a great way of sharing priorities and getting alignment across the team of where help is needed. I will make sure I do it at a time that Pierre can dial in, to include him. I'm sure initially I will get resistance to the idea, but I will tell them it's a 30-day trial, and hopefully, by then, they will see the benefits and buy into it.

'Tell me, Sonya, how would you go about setting the goals and timing of projects where there is a high level of uncertainty, and the design steps are not known in advance?'

'Great question, Chris. For predictive projects, the measures are linked to the known outcomes. If you are involved in an innovation project, the precise steps are unknown, and even the outcome is uncertain. What is certain are the steps within which the innovation happens. For example, you can set a review milestone to define the problem by a set date. The second milestone may be to produce a field trial of your concept by a set date, within a set budget. Leonardi da Vinci said, "Artwork is never finished. Only abandoned." In business, you don't want an innovation project to become a piece of artwork. The management planning milestones ensure that business goals are completed in a set time and within a set budget.'

'Thanks, Sonya, that is helpful. I will make sure I build in these set review markers as part of the measuring phase.'

Chris, as the manager of your team, you also need to review where people are in a broader sense than just the work deliverables and outputs. I suggest you have one-on-one non-operational conversations with each team member at least once a month.' Sonya opened the Leaders Guide and commented on the list of open-ended questions he could ask them.

"Do you know where the company is going?" 'Discuss the big picture, the strategic outlook, etc.

"Where are you going?" 'Discuss their career and development aspects.

"What is going well?" 'Discuss their strengths and successes to build on.

"If you were your own coach, what would you improve?" 'Discuss any lessons learnt and let them own their personal development.

"How can I help you more?" 'Make it safe for your team to give you feedback so that you can adjust your style to get the best out of them.'

Sonya then pointed to a checklist for Chris to read that he could use to check he had implemented effective reporting.

REPORTING CHECKLIST

- Are you continually tracking the results of the plans against measurable outputs and targets?
- Has a regular review process been set up in which to review the measures monthly and quarterly?
- Do all team members do a weekly and monthly report where measures are tracked, and plans and actions converge?

Chris finished reading the list. 'Sonya, I 100% agree with everything you have said, and I would love to meet with my team and do all the things you have mentioned, but to be honest, I don't have the time. I have so many meetings already filling up my day, and when I do meet with my team, the meetings are ineffective and seem to drag on, leaving me with even less time.'

'Chris, focus on quality time with your team. Setting 10 minutes aside of quality time, where you act as though the other person is the only person in the world, beats a long meeting, where you are mentally distracted because of concerns of other priorities. Let us address the quantity of meetings you have.'

Chris gingerly opened his calendar on his smartphone and showed Sonya how the majority of his day was already committed to meetings.

'Wow, that looks pretty intense. I see your point.' Sonya waved her finger at a few of the back-to-back meetings, filling up Chris's precious time.

'Help me understand what these meetings are about,' Sonya asked. 'Why is it essential that you attend these three meetings, for example?'

'To be honest, I have no idea. All these meetings get set up by others, often more senior than me, so I have to attend. I get regularly criticised for my lack of availability because I am so busy, and my boss has told me to work smarter, not harder. He wants me to be accessible to the rest of the business, so the last thing I want to do is reject a meeting invite.'

'So if you spend 80% of your time in meetings, when do you get time to plan for those meetings and address the actions you are assigned in those meetings?'

'Well, that's my problem. I don't. I do all the actions after-hours, and my family is getting pretty frustrated about it, but what else can I do?' Chris sat looking glum and defeated.

Sonya tried to encourage him.

'Chris, a key element of leadership is not to be a victim of your situation. You are not in a popularity contest to see how many people you can please. You are hired to make a difference to the bottom line of the business. Understand why you have been asked to attend those meetings, and then assess the relative priority of those reasons compared to everything else that demands your time.

'Isn't it interesting that anyone can call a meeting with no pre-authorisation? These meetings often cost the business thousands of dollars in travel, meeting rooms, catering, not to mention the opportunity cost of lost time on other things. There is usually an approval process to limit people's authority to spend the company's money on physical items. Yet, there is no pre-approval to call a meeting. With virtual meetings, the barrier to setting up a meeting is even lower, as there are no physical room limitations or travel restrictions. So long as your calendar shows you're free, you can be pulled into any number of meetings, with any number of people, for any time duration with no accountability for the cost to the organisation.

'A useful model to turn meetings from a time-waster into a powerful execution tool is based on the premise that anyone attending a meeting usually has three key thoughts on their mind: Firstly, "What is this all about? Why are we here?" Secondly, "What is going to happen - how is this going to be organised?" And lastly, "Am I really required here - is this worth my time?"

'The model is called PPPP,' said Sonya, pointing to the model in the textbook. 'The acronym is Planning, Purpose, Process, and Payoff.'

Chris studied the model.

PPPP: PLANNING, PURPOSE, PROCESS AND PAYOFF

Planning: To *plan* the meeting for success, ask yourself a few key questions:

- Is a meeting the best method available?
- What will this meeting cost versus the benefits gained?
- How much time is needed? Parkinson's law states that "work expands to fill the time available for its completion." The same is true for meetings, so try making the meetings as short as really necessary.
- What stakeholders need to attend?
- What role do I want each person attending to play?

Purpose: Define the reason for the meeting:

- Ask yourself what the primary purpose is: Is it making decisions, sharing information, solving problems, planning, celebrating success?
- Write down the purpose of the meeting in a single sentence.
- One reason that meetings are ineffective is that the ultimate purpose of the meeting is not clear to everyone at the start of the meeting.

Process: Describe the format to be followed:

- Ask, *'What is going to happen, and how is this going to be organised?'*
- Use an agenda that includes a timed outline of issues covered and lists each attendee's names.
- Attach any pre-meeting reference data, previous minutes, actions, reports or homework, for consideration. This avoids reviewing facts and data in boring PowerPoint slides. Meetings should be for discussion, insights and analysis, not data transfer.

Payoff: Describe the benefits for the people attending:

- Clarify the benefit of all participants dedicating their time to attending the meeting
- When people don't believe they are adding value or receiving value, they will mentally depart the meeting

'Sonya, the PPPP model looks useful, and I will definitely use it for the next meeting I run, but what about when I am invited to the meeting?'

Sonya smiled. 'That's not so easy, is it? As I said earlier, you cannot be a victim of a poorly run or inefficient meeting, as it harms the company. To apply the PPPP process in meetings you attend, ask the meeting organiser the questions listed in the book.' Sonya pointed to the PPPP page in the book. 'Use this PPPP process to check in with the meeting organiser.'

QUESTIONS TO ASK MEETING ORGANISERS

- So that I can add maximum value to this meeting, can I understand why you have invited me?
- If all goes well and exactly to plan, what do you hope to achieve by the end of this meeting?
- Can I check with you, were you hoping for me to contribute, or did you invite me for my benefit?
- Is there an agenda I can review so I can see what is planned for this meeting?

'Nice.' Chris said. 'I suppose once you have answers to those questions, you can assess the relative priority of what was going to occupy your time.'

He thanked Sonya for her valuable insights and advice and promised himself that by the time they met again, he would clear at least half of his calendar of meetings where he was not adding sufficient value and headed home.

20

PEOPLE AND PERSONALITIES

It was 8.10 on Monday morning, and the coffee shop was a hive of activity. Chris slumped into the chair opposite Sonya.

'Sorry I am late. I need a triple shot of coffee today. Kids! Where am I going wrong? You bring your kids up the same, and they have the same family genes, so why don't they all *behave* in the same way?

'Liam always leaves things to the last minute. He came to me at 8pm last night and casually mentioned that he has a school project where he needs a lunchbox. Not just *any* lunch box. This lunch box has to be a specific size and made with specific material because they plan to gouge holes in it. The lunchbox is only available in a speciality store, as mentioned in a school letter issued last Tuesday, which he unhelpfully pulled from the bottom of his bag last night! So, I had to rush to the store on the opposite side of town to get this lunchbox before dropping the kids at school. Sorry to rant. I don't understand why Liam can't be more like Nathan. Even though Nat is two years younger, he would have asked for the lunchbox on Saturday afternoon when we were near the store.'

Chris realised he had added further delays to his meeting with Sonya and so composed himself and asked, 'So what are we talking about this week?'

Sonya paused, wondering whether she should go back to his home story, but moved on for now, as she was confident that he would make the link back to personalities when they addressed that topic later on.

They started walking back towards the office. Sonya looked forward to the day she would ask Chris what was top of mind for him, rather than him expecting her to set the priorities, but she realised he still needed some direction.

'Chris, this week, I would like to understand what lessons you have learned about the good and bad of Taylor's management methods and how it applies to the diverse group of people in your team.'

They sat down at the conference table. Chris spoke first. 'You asked what lessons I learnt from Taylor, so here goes.

'Taylor worked out how to make a process efficient by taking the thinking element out of the *doing* phase. Compared to the "tricks-of-the-trade" methods, his "one right way" produced far better results. The benefit of his planning methodology is that he took the best methods and standardised them to achieve repeatable results to a consistent standard.

'The downside of compliance standards is that they inhibit the *best* worker. In Taylor's day, his average worker may have produced better results than the industry average, but it stifled creativity and innovation for the best worker.

'I think my "aha moment" is that I need to re-humanise the workplace. Managing teams is mainly about managing people, not things. I think I will crack the formula to managing and leading high-performing teams if I unleash the brilliance and creativity of the people while also using processes to get consistent, repeatable results.'

Sonya looked impressed. Chris had come a long way from when she first met him, where he had tried to convince her that "soft skills" were just for HR departments.

'I have to live in the real world,' he had said back then, 'and in the real world, it's about facts and data, not about feelings and emotions.'

Sonya brought her mind back to the present. 'Chris, that was a good summary. Notice the contradiction and paradox. In engineering, there is often one right way to do things. In management, two seemingly opposite approaches can both be right. The trick is to get the right balance between the two approaches and apply the right option to the right situation.

'We want people to behave in habitual and repeatable ways, and we also want them to be innovative and flexible. You cannot program a person to perform as though they were a robot.

'People have a set of preferences, which may be different to yours. Even with *personally* defined preferences, there is no hard-wired formula, as people are not even sure themselves about how they tick. Take me, for example. At a restaurant, I love to eat fish, but occasionally I prefer steak. I do not understand why or when. But some days I order steak, much to the surprise of my partner who thinks he *knows* me. An eating preference model would define me as a dominant fish eater rather than a steak eater. As a *fish-eating-type,* my preferences could be correctly predicted for 80% of the time, which may be helpful in certain circumstances. A limitation of the model is that it would be wrong 20% of the time.

'We all have a totally unique personality and can adapt our views and preferences at different times and in different situations, at will. Personality typecasting models help us analyse people's personalities, and these models can help us understand our general preferences. Still, they do not define how we feel about every situation and do not necessarily determine how we behave.

'I'll leave you to read the chapter on people and personality types. When would you like to meet again?'

Chris thumbed through his calendar planner. 'How about Thursday next week?'

Sonya confirmed the appointment and departed.

That evening Chris continued to read *The Leaders Guide* book.

PEOPLE AND PERSONALITY TYPES

People are complex creatures and totally unique. However, for thousands of years, we have known that groups of people have common characteristics. Some people seem more outgoing than others. Some people love adrenalin-fuelled risk-taking; others do not. Some people are organised and care deeply about being on time, while others regard disorganisation as creativity. Some people seek crystal-clear clarity on matters, while others appear to be happy with ambiguity and are very comfortable with shades of grey.

To get the best out of people, a manager needs to adapt their leadership style to the people they are working with. Treating everyone the same way, or treating people in the way we like to be treated, can backfire as each person has a unique perspective.

The Greek doctor Hippocrates, in 440 BC, defined four temperaments based on his misunderstanding of body fiuids. He called these humors, and divided his patients into four fiuid categories that, in his view, explained their behaviour patterns based on four personality temperaments: choleric, sanguine, melancholic, and phlegmatic. Plato and Aristotle each had *their* personality theories, and interestingly also had four categories.

In 1921 *Carl Jung* published *"Psychological Types"* where he describes how he categorised his psychiatry patients to predict their behaviour and provide standardised treatments. He defined three pairs of preferences: Extravert/Introvert (EI), Sensor/Intuitor (SN) and Thinker/Feeler (TF).

Katharine Briggs and her daughter *Isabel Briggs Myers* adapted Jung's model during World War II to help assess where women would be best placed in wartime jobs and added a fourth pair: Judger / Perceiver (JP). The Myers Briggs Type Indicator (MBTI) and the Management Team Roles-Indicator (MTR-i) helps assess behavioural preferences.

There are many quadrant-based personality models used in the workplace, such as Merrill-Reid, Keirsey, Marston's (DISC), and more recently, Deloitte. Some are based on colour differences, others on animal types and others, such as the Enneagram, have nine interconnected types. Each one claims to be better than the rest. The overriding principle in all these models is that misunderstandings can happen based on two people seeing an identical situation with two opposite perspectives.

Personality profiling defines preferences and is not a predictor of actual behaviour. There is also no preferred personality type because your type is not an indicator of intellectual or emotional ability or performance.

In psychology, five major personality traits are defined – these are sometimes called the Big 5. OCEAN is used as a memory jogger: Openness, Conscientiousness, Extraversion, Agreeableness, and Neuroticism.

Openness to experience refers to the degree of being adventurous, creative, and having a range of interests. How open are we to new ideas? People low on the Openness scale are more traditional, resist change and struggle with abstract thinking.

People with a high degree of Conscientiousness are goal-oriented with good impulse control. They are diligent, dependable, and dutiful. People low on the Conscientiousness scale dislike structure and are impulsive and spontaneous.

Extraversion describes the level to which people are energised by interacting with people. Strong extraverts talk in order to think. People low on the Extraversion scale are energised by solitude, dislike small talk and can find it stressful starting conversations with new people.

Agreeableness is the extent to which people trust others, are kind and helpful and have high empathy. Those low on the Agreeableness scale have little interest in others and can manipulate others for self-gain. They can be argumentative and competitive.

Neuroticism is the degree to which people are easily stressed, worry a lot, get easily upset and struggle to bounce back from emotional upsets. Someone low on the Neuroticism scale is not easily alarmed or concerned by their environment. They go about their business with little worry about negative consequences.

In the workplace, clashes in personality types can inhibit team performance. People high on the extraversion scale can easily dominate a conversation in their eagerness to contribute. This behaviour is often regarded as self-centred or rude by those who are low in extraversion. People who are slow to speak can be misjudged as having nothing to contribute, or worse still, deliberately withholding their contributions. People who are analytical and value objective data to make decisions can be seen as cold-hearted or lacking intuition by those with the opposite personality. Those who are more risk-averse can be perceived as negative because they focus on the things that can go wrong.

Neuroscience has shown that, depending on our personalities, information follows different neural paths and stimulates different hormones. The same situation that is extremely exciting and enjoyable for one person can be stressful to another.

War veteran Don Clifton started the global Strengths movement when he asked the question, "What would happen if we studied what was right with people versus what's wrong with people?" In 2007, Tom Rath's book *StrengthsFinder 2.0* was published. The concept of the Gallup CliftonStrengths model is that we all have 34 strengths, organised into four categories: Executing, Infiuencing, Relationship Building and Strategic Thinking. Each strength has a balcony where it works for you and a basement where the strength is not helpful and needs to be toned down. Teams can be analysed for their mix of strengths and skills insourced where a team lacks a key strength in a particular category.

APPLYING TYPECASTING
AT WORK

Chris reflected on what he had read. Personality differences were the root cause of a lot of negative conflict in the business, but Chris had always tried, without success, to *change* the people who were different to him. It now occurred to Chris that he may have misinterpreted the motives of others based on *his* interpretation of their behaviours. Chris anticipated an interesting session with Sonya to explore this more deeply.

On Thursday, Chris was in his office when he looked at his watch and realised he was due to meet Sonya for his regular catch-up. He virtually ran to the meeting room. Chris smiled at himself, realising that his personality drove his behaviour. He hated being late. To him, it was rude and an indication of being disorganised and unreliable.

Chris got straight to the point. 'Sonya, I have found all this material about personalities fascinating. I have done both the Myers Briggs and DISC personality tests more than once, and while I definitely identify with the models, I am not convinced that typecasting works.

'I got different results when I took the tests at different times in my career. Surely the results depend on the situation? For example, at work, I am more extraverted, as I meet with people and spend most of my day talking, but I am more introverted at home. The test is based on a set of questions, and the results I get, depend on which examples I reference when I answer these questions.'

Sonya laughed. 'Back in 1948, Bertram Forer did a personality test experiment, where he made participants take a test and then read their results to them. People were stunned by how well he had described them until Forer pointed out that everyone was given the same feedback. He had cleverly provided generic statements like, "you have a great need for other people to like and admire you," which played on a psychological trait called *confirmation bias*. This is a bias where people distort objective data to value information more highly that supports what they already believe to be true. So yes, you are right. These tests are open to distortions and unconscious bias and manipulation.

'These personality-type schemes take something which is very complex and reduce it down to a binary score. For example, in Myers Briggs typecasting, 0-49% extraversion is deemed I (introvert), and 51-100% extraversion is deemed E (extravert). If one person was 52% Extravert, and another was 85% extravert, both would be categorised as E (extravert), and hence would be expected to have the same preferences. In reality, a 52% Extravert would have far more in common with a 48% Introvert than with the 85% Extravert.

'Typecasting is not an exact science. The main point of me getting you to study *typecasting* is to recognise that we all have different personality styles and preferences. There is no right or wrong personality, but there are certain behaviours necessary for different circumstances. Typecasting helps us understand ourselves and others better.'

'I think I get it.' said Chris. 'So instead of telling the extrovert to stop being rude and interrupting people, you could investigate why that was their default behaviour. Focussing on the positive motive to contribute and understanding how energised they were by the interaction would help when delivering the feedback about the impact of their behaviour.'

'Exactly. Some people may never understand why you care so much about starting meetings on time, but you can get alignment and agreement that everyone should be on time for your meeting, whether or not it comes naturally to them.

'Understanding typecasting helps us to develop more empathy, to see things from the perspective of the other person and not assume that everyone sees things the same way that we do. You need to recognise that certain activities are far more stressful and unpleasant for some team members than others.

'Chris, you are not required to *fix* the team members' personalities but to help them develop appropriate behaviours that are required in different circumstances.

'Be careful not to use personality typecasting as a form of discrimination. The *nurture* versus *nature* argument rages on. There is evidence that we are born with a certain personality type. Also, our environment - especially the relationship with our primary caregiver at an early age - plays a dominant role. Some psychologists argue that our personality is set by the age of seven. If this is true, I think it is discriminatory to judge someone based on their personality type.'

'I agree,' said Chris. 'Maybe one way of thinking about it is that each of us has a different size and colour elastic band. We can stretch the band in different circumstances. Over the years, based on our life's experiences, we can stretch the band, but our comfort zone is the unstretched band, based primarily on our genes and early development. Stretching the band by *adapting* our behaviour to achieve our goals and being comfortable with who we are when in an unstretched state is part of having a mature personality.'

'Exactly,' said Sonya. 'Use typecasting to understand *yourself*. This is the first step to understanding others. Understanding others will help you understand how they may *prefer* you to deal with them.'

Chris hesitated. 'Sonya, the person I have the most trouble with is Pierre. How would typecasting help?'

'Okay, let's see if we can do a quick analysis of your personality differences.'

'Well, I am quite introverted. I enjoy being with people, but too much interaction drains me. I am analytical. I like data to be presented sequentially and in writing. I make decisions based on reason and logic, not feelings. I am a bit of a stickler for being on time. Lastly, I strongly believe in doing what I say I will do.'

'And Pierre?'

'Well, he is very extraverted. In my opinion, he operates too much on gut instinct. He makes decisions based on his feelings. Timekeeping is something that doesn't bother him, and he loves ambiguity. He seems to find it impossible to make decisions because he always thinks of new ideas and options instead of deciding on the options on the table.'

'Chris, your regular clashes may be because you both see the world from different perspectives. Pierre is the exact opposite type to you. His view may be that you do not use your gut instinct enough and that you ignore people's feelings when making decisions. He probably thinks you are *too* inflexible and *too* analytical.

'Instead of debating who is right, try to adapt your style to align to his preferences. You might find you get better results that way. Allow him to talk freely, to gather his thoughts. Have a conversation rather than using email to share data. Consider his feelings when making decisions and give him space to explore and express his ideas before judging them.'

'Thanks, those are helpful insights, Sonya.'

'You're welcome. Typecasting is very helpful in understanding motivation too. Read up on that in the textbook, and we will cover it in our session next week.'

With that, Sonya packed up her things and departed.

Chris headed back to the office and almost literally bumped into Chuck, the sales and marketing director, who was bounding down the hallway with his usual exuberant pace.

'Got a minute, Chris?'

Chuck grabbed Chris by the arm and led him into a nearby vacant meeting room.

'Listen, buddy, I rarely interfere, but your team is starting to drive me a little crazy, and I may need your help.'

'Sure, Chuck,' said Chris, avoiding eye contact. 'What's the problem?'

'Well, we had a meeting with Portico, which as you know is one of our top clients. They are having a myriad of technical issues with the product, so we took a couple of your engineers into the meeting, and they were hopeless.' Chuck paused for effect.

'Hopeless. They kept asking a bunch of detailed technical questions and sat there, silently writing notes instead of coming up with suggestions of how to fix the customer issue. Every time my sales lead tried to reassure the customer of what we would do to fix this, they would contradict him, leaving the client with no hope of a solution. Chris, your team do not seem to care about the customer. All they care about is their geeky technology.'

In the past, Chris would have been either defensive or gone into attack mode, but Sonya had been coaching him to *understand before judging.*

'Thanks for updating me, Chuck. Let me investigate the situation, and I will get back to you by the end of the day.'

Chris went straight to his team to discuss the problem.

'I believe we met with Portico today, and I hear they are having technical issues with the product. My understanding is we have not resolved the issues yet, and the sales team seems disappointed that we did not offer any assurances or solutions in the meeting. Can someone fill me in with the details from your perspective? I need to get back to Chuck with a recommendation.'

As the technical lead for the Portico account, Madison spoke first. 'We were not told that Portico was visiting today and were dragged into this meeting to explain how we were going to fix their problems. I hate it when salespeople do that to us. We could not prepare anything or even look up which software version they are running. The way they have configured the solution is different to our other clients, and there are a hundred different reasons why they could be experiencing those problems, many of which may have nothing to do with us.'

Fred continued. 'Madison is right. Portico insists they want to control their own release schedule, using their own testing regime, but they never tell us when rollover day is. We have been asking the sales team for months to address this with them because then we could help. Instead, they drag us into a meeting with no warning, and we look like a bunch of gooses. In the meeting, sales kept promising the customer things we cannot deliver. Sales do not seem to care about the customer. All they care about is their commission cheque.'

Chris listened carefully as the team shared their frustrations and then helped them define the next steps, with clear ownership of who would do *what*, by *when*.

Chris said he would share the plan with Chuck and closed the meeting.

Later that day, while driving home, he considered how much personalities frame our interpretation of the motives of others. Clearly, the people in both sales and engineering cared deeply about the customer, yet each judged the other through their own personality lens.

UNDERSTANDING MOTIVATION

Nathan was sitting in the den busily creating a Lego megacity. Liam was lying on the couch with headphones on, his thumbs furiously working the controls of a computer game. Evelyn sat at the piano, practising her piano scales. Gwen had started making dinner, and some delicious smells were wafting into the living room from the kitchen. 'Just a typical evening,' Chris thought, pleased to be a family man.

Just then, something starkly interrupted his thoughts... discordant piano sounds. Chris went to investigate.

Evelyn was bashing both hands on the keys in perfect unison while moving up and down the octaves like a two-year-old, wailing, 'I... hate... the... piano.'

Chris held both wrists in suspension above the piano to call a halt to this dreadful noise. 'Eve, we talked about this before. You don't hate the piano. You always say how much you love the piano. Just last week, when you reviewed the videos I have been making of you playing, you told me how much you have improved. What is the problem this time?'

'Dad, I am sick of it. I spend all my time practising boring scales or working on the hardest bits of my music score, and so it never feels like any fun.'

Chris knew how much she loved playing her set-pieces once she had perfected them, and he also knew she had a gift for music. It would be tragic if she gave up now. He also understood it would be hard to put in so much effort for so little short-term reward.

'Evelyn, to excel at something, you have to put in lots of hard work. The reward for all that hard work and dedication comes later when you see the structural improvements. You need to balance that with short-term rewards.

'You've been practising for ages now. Why not play a few of your favourite songs, just for fun?'

Chris headed off to the kitchen as he was making a baked dessert to follow the main course that Gwen was preparing. A few minutes later, a broad smile came over his face when he heard the sounds of laughter over a piano duet. He popped his head into the lounge to see what was going on. Liam was sitting at the piano with Evelyn. The two of them were laughing and playing a silly song that looked more like a game of Twister than a piano duet.

Evelyn turned to face him, grinning. 'Dad, I love the piano.'

Later that evening, Chris settled down to read his Leaders Guide, still reflecting on Evelyn's lesson in motivation.

UNDERSTANDING MOTIVATION

We are all motivated by different things based on our personal circumstances and individual personalities.

Abraham Maslow, in his 1943 paper, *A Theory of Human Motivation*, suggested there are five stages of satisfying human need. The diagram below illustrates these five stages.

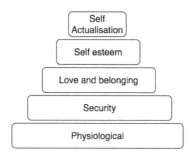

Maslow postulated that people would not be motivated by a higher-level need until they sufficiently satisfy the lower-level need. Senior managers, who sit at the top of the needs pyramid, often misunderstand the motivational drives of more junior staff. A Gen Y team member struggling to afford the mortgage for their house may sacrifice favourable job conditions for a job with higher pay.

The management team at Hawthorne Works, a Western Electric factory, did a series of lighting experiments in the 1920s to see the impact on production efficiency. They temporarily upgraded the lighting, and production improved. Surprisingly, when the temporary lighting was removed, production improved once again. It appears the management's attention to worker conditions improved the production levels, rather than the changes in lighting conditions. With motivation, any management interest and attention is better than none. The impact of being observed, and its effect on behaviour, is now called the **Hawthorne effect.**

Jim Collins, author of *Good to Great* (2001), makes an interesting observation about motivation. "The best people don't work purely for money: they will wake up in the morning already engaged. Successful leaders don't spend much time motivating people: they get self-motivated people around them and give them a lot of freedom within a framework of responsibilities. But even self-motivated and self-disciplined people can become demotivated if they believe they are in an environment where people don't want to face the facts; if they see that they are carrying the weight of other people or if they feel they are in a failing organisation."

The late Frederick Herzberg, an American psychologist, was one of the most influential people in developing management theory regarding motivation.

He identified two factors that impact motivation. Extrinsic and Intrinsic factors:

* **Extrinsic factors** - also called Hygiene factors. These external factors such as working conditions, company policy, pay and job security can demotivate staff, but they do not necessarily motivate. Improvements in external factors can reduce demotivation but do not increase long-term motivation. At best, extrinsic factors have a short-term impact on motivation.
* **Intrinsic factors** - also called Motivators. These are related to the job itself - the level of responsibility, feelings of achievement and personal growth. These factors can truly motivate.

In 1960, Douglas McGregor published a book called *The Human Side of Enterprise*. He suggested that managers have two strong but opposing life views that influence their management styles. He called those managers who believed workers were inherently lazy and required external motivation, Theory X managers. Theory Y managers believe that most people are motivated to work and will direct and control themselves. The way managers treat their staff is assumed to be linked to whether they are Theory X or Y believers.

Managers often get frustrated that they have little control over extrinsic factors, such as salaries and company policy, but these things are not motivators. Working in a team can satisfy several needs, such as security, love and belonging, and even self-esteem. The way the team leader interacts with the team and handles the people dynamics makes all the difference to whether someone feels like they are human capital and a *resource* or feels part of a human *tribe* that works together collaboratively for a common and worthwhile goal.

Managers can influence intrinsic factors by creating an

environment where motivation can flourish. Company exit surveys show that people leave managers rather than companies.

REAL WORLD MOTIVATORS

In Daniel Pink's book *Drive* (2009), he refers to three primary psychological drives - autonomy, purpose, and mastery.

Self-determination theory (SDT) defines the three drives as autonomy, relatedness, and competence.

Applying these psychological drives in human nature to managing a team addresses things that significantly impact motivation. Most externally driven schemes to motivate smart people fail because they do not address these fundamental human qualities.

Chris finished reading about SDT and reflected on what lessons he could apply to his technical team at work. He wrote some notes.

- *Give my team autonomy. They love figuring out 'the how'*
- *Make the team feel included and recognise their contributions*
- *Ask more questions and seek out their opinions*
- *Show an interest in their work*
- *Include them in broader company issues*
- *Listen to understand, not respond*
- *Show they are valued for who they are, not just what they do*
- *Help them to grow their knowledge and master their skills*

Chris put down the notebook and walked to the kitchen to get himself a glass of water before going to bed.

'Liam!' he moaned as he stared at the dirty kitchen floor. Chris and Gwen gave each of their children chores to do in return for extra pocket money. He looked across at the kitchen sink. Evelyn had washed all the dishes, stacked them, and wiped down the countertops so that they sparkled. Nathan was only 8, and yet he had completed his task flawlessly. The condiments on the dining table were cleared away, and everything was set ready for breakfast. All Liam had to do was mop the kitchen floor.

'How hard can it be?' Chris muttered as he walked over to collect the mop, having an imaginary argument with Liam about deducting money from his weekly pocket money allowance.

Chris knew he was discussing team motivation with Sonya in his next session. He decided to get some advice for dealing with his home situation.

WHY ARE YOU NOT MOTIVATED LIKE ME

Chris and Sonya settled down in the meeting room.

'Any chance you can adjust the air-conditioning?' Sonya asked.

Chris smiled and reached for the remote control. The room temperature was a source of constant battles.

'Sure, but the room temperature feels fine to me. Are you too hot or too cold?'

'Too cold. This room is freezing.'

'Okay, I've turned it up by 2 degrees. The room should heat up soon.

'Sonya, I read the theories in the book about motivation and understood it, but I am still confused why some of my team are motivated and others aren't. To be honest, I have the same issue at home with my kids.'

Sonya leaned forward with a serious look on her face. 'Chris, everyone is motivated. Some people are just not motivated in the way *you* want them to be. Give me an example of someone you feel is not motivated.'

'Let's take Fred. He is an excellent worker and has been here for years, but he always seems so negative about new ideas. Just today, I suggested we scrap our qualification gating sheet as it is slowing down progress. Immediately Fred gives 50 reasons why it is a bad idea. He was around when they first introduced it, and he reckons that all those old problems will come back if we scrap the qualification sheet. He is so negative and blocks us from moving forward with any changes.'

'Chris, consider for a minute what the motive is for Fred *being negative*. He sees risks you do not see, and he is trying to protect the business from failure. That sounds like a pretty motivated guy to me. The difference is that you are motivated to change the system to improve the business, and he is motivated to *stop* the change to improve the business. Your outlook is focused on the opportunity for improvement, and Fred's outlook is focused on avoiding risk.'

'Sonya, I think I get it. Fred is not a bad guy, but I feel like he doesn't respect me. I am aware of all his experience, and even if he doesn't verbally challenge me, I feel like he is judging me.'

'Chris, the way to get respect is to give respect. Fred may feel that you do not value his experience and you are more important than him because you are the manager. Show him the respect for his experience and contributions, and I believe he will reciprocate.'

'I have never thought of it that way. Thanks, Sonya. When I meet with Fred, I will ask him to tell me more about why he is *motivated* to keep the qualification sheet. I will make him aware that I respect him because I do. Maybe there *is* something I am missing.'

Chris paused and then offered a second example. 'Another person I struggle with sometimes is Rodrigues. Usually, he is very motivated, but he can also be up and down. Some days he appears fired up, and then, for no apparent reason, he suddenly becomes quiet and despondent. For example, last week, he came to show me a new product interface he had designed. He was buzzing. I didn't have time to hear about the technical details, but I told him how amazing he was and how much I appreciated him. Despite all my positive words, he left looking demotivated, which left me confused.'

Sonya could see Chris genuinely did not know how he had contributed to the situation, so she offered an analogy. 'Chris, you told me you have three children. Can you remember the day Evelyn was born?'

Chris felt emotion well up inside him as he recalled the proud moment he had witnessed the birth of his firstborn. Evelyn had no hair when she was born with splotchy red marks from birth trauma. Yet he remembered thinking she was the most beautiful thing he had ever seen. 'Of course I recall that.'

'And how would you feel if I congratulated you but showed no interest in your new baby? No interest in the baby's sex, no interest in the name, no interest in the weight, no interest in your wife's birth experience. I am guessing my congratulatory words would mean nothing to you.

'To technical people, their project is *their baby*. When you say you are only interested in the end results with no interest in *how* they achieved that result, it can be very demotivating. Of course, you do not have time to understand *all* the technical details, but if you want to make sure you do not demotivate technical people, be interested in the details.'

Chris shook his head in disbelief at how he had missed that. 'You know I get that all the time with *my* management. As a technical person, I am proud of the creative thinking and innovation we display to produce solutions, but no one seems interested. I cannot believe I have made the same mistake with Rodrigues.'

Sonya continued. 'You mentioned you were having similar issues at home with your kids. Tell me more about that.'

Chris told Sonya all about Liam. His final statement was, 'the kid just doesn't care. Seriously, he is totally unmotivated. It doesn't matter what we try.'

'What does Liam *like* doing?'

'Playing computer games.'

'So Liam is a motivated kid. It motivates him to play computer games rather than wash the kitchen floor. He probably doesn't care about the kitchen floor. It may genuinely make no difference in his life whether the kitchen floor has crumbs on it, and possibly the extra money you give him is not worth the sacrifice of reduced time playing computer games with his mates.

'To fully understand motivation, understand it from the other person's perspective, not yours.

'Look at the work situation. Not all people have the same motivations as mine. I may assume that everyone would be motivated by an all-expenses-paid golfing weekend, just because I would love it. But some people may hate golf. You, for example, may love golf, but you may value spending time with your family *more* than being sent off on a business golfing event, no matter how luxurious it was.'

Chris grinned. 'It depends. What sort of luxury are we talking about here?'

Sonya smiled. 'Recognition plays a huge part in motivation. Giving someone money when they crave recognition may not have the expected impact. Recognition is often as important as the reward itself. Therefore, *how* the reward is given is essential. While genuine praise from a senior manager is likely to have a positive impact, a *let's recognise-the-staff* program will often backfire, as intelligent people can become cynical of the true motives of these schemes. Recognition and rewards work best when customized to the needs of individual members of the team.

'Most people want to feel they are making a difference, that they are part of something exciting, and that their contribution matters. Many managers try to increase motivation by *protecting* their staff from complex tasks beyond their experience levels or may exclude them from key meetings that they may feel are too demanding. Ironically, it is often this very work that would have the biggest impact on their motivation. High performing people are motivated by challenges, not an easy life.'

Chris listened carefully and agreed that challenges motivated his best people, but he had one person who *did* want an easy life at work. 'Fred is not too far off retirement, and these days, his motivations are definitely not in the office.' He also pointed out that understanding Liam's motivations still didn't get the floor mopped.

'So, how do I deal with that?' Chris asked, throwing his hands up.

Sonya pointed at Chris's textbook. 'It's all in the next section. Keep reading, and we can discuss how to deal with managing poor performance in our next session.

'I'm parched. Do you fancy joining me for a coffee on my way out?'

'You bet. I'll never say no to a coffee.'

At the cafe, Chris and Sonya were engaged in light-hearted conversation when they were interrupted by a customer complaining in a loud voice. 'I had to walk around the entire block to find the coffee shop because the sign was facing the wrong way.'

The owner turned to the barista. 'I asked you to put out the sign this morning. Did you point it in the shop's direction?'

'I am not sure,' the barista responded. 'My priority was to get to work and prepare the coffee machine. I didn't have time to check the orientation, and anyway, our regular customers already know where we are. I was asked to put out the sign, so I did. Nobody told me to point it towards the coffee shop.'

'Well, can you go immediately and turn it the right way round,' the owner said.

'Sure, but what about all these customers who are waiting for their coffee?'

Begrudgingly, the owner told the barista to carry on making coffee. As the owner left to adjust the sign, he shouted into the wind, 'Why am I never able to hire competent staff? Why do *I* always end up having to do everything?'

As his voice faded into the traffic noise, the barista looked somewhat embarrassed. He restored his dignity by pointing to his *Barista of the Year* certificate proudly hanging on the wall and announced to the remaining customers, 'I think we all know who is the incompetent one.' With that, he concentrated intensely on his coffee making.

Chris raised an eyebrow as he looked at Sonya, who was by now standing and ready to depart. 'It's amazing how similar the challenges are in my engineering world to those experienced in this cafe, isn't it, Sonya?'

Chris decided that he, too, needed to get back to work. He had a meeting lined up with Rodrigues, and based on what he had learnt about motivation, Chris planned to listen carefully before offering any opinions.

Rodrigues was a junior engineer who had joined the team relatively recently. His work was outstanding, and he was very bright. Chris really liked him. His fundamental weakness was that he did not collaborate. In the past few weeks, Rodrigues seemed demotivated, so Chris was pleased about the meeting. He wanted to find out what was going on.

'Hi Chris, thanks for meeting with me.'

'Sure, Rodrigues. I am very happy with your work and love having you on the team. I have noticed in the past few weeks that you don't seem like your usual cheerful self. I want to understand what is troubling you and whether there is anything I can do to help.'

'Well, to be honest, I have been a bit upset at the way the team reacted to an idea I had. I noticed some problems with our current process and took the initiative to improve it. I worked half the night on upgrading the process, and instead of praise, the team criticised me for not talking to them first before implementing the improvements. It seems they have a not-invented-here mindset.'

Chris recognised that Rodrigues had completely missed the point about collaboration and thought he could help the team out by explaining it with more authority.

'Rodrigues, I am sure the team is grateful for your hard work, but you should have discussed your idea with them first. You are relatively new to the team, and yet you have gone around them by implementing your new idea with no collaboration. I didn't even know you had changed the process. Can you understand that what you did was wrong?'

Rodrigues looked at the floor and said nothing.

'Rodrigues, do you agree with me?'

'Yes, you're right. I am sorry.'

Rodrigues left the meeting and called a friend.

'... and then my boss took their side. They talk about innovation, but they don't want change. That's the last time I go above-and-beyond to volunteer to improve something.'

As Chris drove home from work, he felt pleased that he had spoken his mind about something that had been eating away at him. But he had doubts. 'What am I missing? I wonder how I could have handled that situation better?'

MOTIVATING ABOVE AND BELOW THE COMPLIANCE LINE

Sonya surveyed the driving range, then inserted a few coins into the vending machine, and 50 golf balls came clattering down into the strategically placed bucket at the end of the chute. Her beautiful *Cobra King F6* driver was tucked neatly under her arm as she made her way to an empty lane.

She hit a dozen balls into the distance and then stopped to review her swing. Moving in slow motion, she repeated what she had learnt in her last lesson at a painstakingly slow speed while hitting an imaginary ball on the ground. She repeated the movement until she felt she had perfected it and then placed an actual golf ball on the rubber tee before hitting it with laser precision into a predetermined location.

To end her session on the driving range, Sonya smashed the last dozen balls as far as she could, just for fun. She had learnt that to achieve mastery you need to enjoy the journey.

Satisfied with her practice session, Sonya went home. It was the weekend, and she planned to continue reading up on exactly how the set of 14 golf clubs that was the maximum number allowed to be in your bag were made up. Technically, what was the difference between a nine iron and a seven iron? When do you use a wood versus an iron club? What were the more complex rules, such as replacing a lost ball? Sonya had learnt that for mastery, there are a few key ingredients:

- A deep theoretical understanding of the subject
- Practical application of the concepts
- The right mindset
- Practise to form new habits

Meanwhile, Chris had settled down with his book and turned to the next chapter.

MANAGING ABOVE AND BELOW THE LINE

Psychologists had long believed that all primates are driven by one of two things: a *biological* drive; or an *external* drive. *Daniel Pink*, the author of *Drive: the surprising truth about what motivates us* (2009), points to the discovery of a third drive. This third drive, our *intrinsic* drive, is the desire to do something just for the pleasure of doing it. The interesting thing about the research is that adding the *external* drive - rewards and punishment - to an *intrinsically motivating activity* has a detrimental effect. If someone is already intrinsically motivated to do something, the promise of a reward or threat of punishment actually decreases performance rather than increasing it further.

If someone is not intrinsically motivated to do something, extrinsic motivation is needed. If we apply extrinsic motivation to someone already intrinsically motivated, we make the situation worse, not better.

A useful framework to help guide us through this apparent paradox is shown in the diagram below:

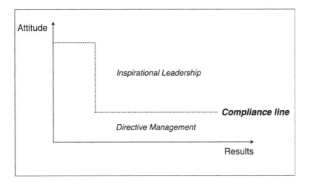

The vertical dotted line represents the minimum acceptable performance. To the left of this vertical line, the skills are not yet competent. To the right of this vertical line, the person is striving for mastery.

The horizontal dotted line represents the minimum acceptable behaviour, which is driven by their attitude. Below the horizontal dotted line, the behaviour is unacceptable and should not be tolerated.

The compliance line defines the minimum standards in terms of results and motivation. *Below this line,* the management style needs to be directive to ensure that the minimum results are achieved. The carrot-stick approach works because the output is clearly defined, and the means to achieve it is known. *Above the line,* inspirational leadership is required. By matching the management style to be directive or supportive, depending on the compliance line, allows a manager to achieve the best of both worlds.

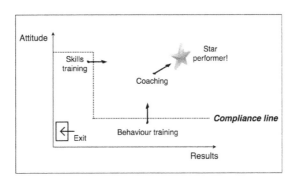

If someone has both unacceptable results and an unacceptable attitude, it is probably best to *exit* them from the business. You cannot coach or teach someone who does not want to improve.

At the opposite end of that scale, the *star* has an outstanding attitude and produces great results. It is essential not to ignore stars. Otherwise, they may become complacent. Stars rarely need support or help, and when it is offered, they can become offended. What they need is inspiration to keep raising the bar. Stay connected, and challenge stars.

If someone lacks skills but has a good attitude, *training* is recommended. Behaviour-management training is needed for someone producing excellent results but with a poor attitude and toxic behaviour. If this does not change their behaviour, it is best to exit them as a toxic culture affects overall team results, even if the specific results of the individual are good.

Where people are already operating above the line, or where innovation is involved, by its very nature, the method is unknown, so it is impossible for a manager to enforce an outcome with the carrot-stick approach. Attempts to do so usually backfire, just as Pink predicted because it takes all the enjoyment and creative thinking out of the solution. Above the line, people are already motivated and have the skills to perform. What they need are support and encouragement. Be a good listener and stimulate the intrinsic motivation that is already there.

Chris reflected on his meeting with Rodrigues. Rodrigues was very competent at his job and also hard working. He had volunteered to do something extra, so he was clearly operating above the compliance line.

Rodrigues, a motivated engineer, had been demotivated by an apparent lack of support from his team. Chris realised that his *directive performance* lecture about collaboration was the last thing that would motivate Rodrigues.

Chris thought about the motivation model. This was an *above-the-compliance-line* situation. He could have used a supportive and encouraging coaching style of management by validating his innovative suggestion. If Rodrigues felt valued and appreciated, any discussion about increased collaboration would have gone down far better.

Chris made an entry in his day planner to see Rodrigues the following day, as he wanted to apologise and give him some encouragement. He also wanted to discuss with Sonya how he could apply the compliance model more generally. Chris grinned devilishly. 'Maybe I can use this model with Liam and the kitchen floor.'

PERFORMANCE MANAGEMENT

Chris was in the middle of a performance review conversation with Fred.

'Fred, I do not understand why you are so upset with your evaluation. I have said you are a solid performer, and you have a 3 rating. That is good. We have a forced ranking system where only 10% of the team can be marked as a 1 (exceptional) with a further 20% as 2 (exceeds expectations).'

Fred was shaking his head slowly from side to side and looking down at the evaluation form. 'So, I am a 3 - meets criteria. Would you say when I voluntarily stayed behind last Friday night for that customer crisis that I just 'met the criteria?'

Chris became flustered. 'Look, the evaluation is not based on one event. I know you do go above-and-beyond sometimes, but your overall performance is statistically average. It's just how the scoring works out. I told you I am happy with how things are going. I have seen improvements recently.'

The conversation went round and round in circles, with neither party enjoying the outcome.

Chris left to meet up with Sonya.

'Sonya, I have been thinking about motivation in the context of *performance management.* I think I am a Theory Y manager in McGregor's model. I believe that most people inherently want to do a good job and do not need constant external intervention, but it seems performance management schemes are designed as extrinsic motivators. Most performance schemes are normalised and aligned to the 50% median, leaving the majority of people feeling demotivated by the scheme. KPI's, almost by definition, are linked to the compliance line and therefore cannot be used to assess above-the-line performance, where people have gone above-and-beyond.'

Sonya replied. 'Chris, you are *so* right, and for this very reason, many companies, particularly technical ones, have gone away from this forced ranking system. Instead, they have meaningful forward-looking conversations to discuss performance. Promotions and financial rewards are determined through a rich set of qualitative and quantitative data points, not just through an objective data-centric performance review.

'The way the feedback is given in a performance review is also critical if it is to be motivational. It may be statistically true to tell a team member that they are *average*, but it is not likely to be motivating.'

Chris shifted uncomfortably in his chair.

'Helpful feedback provides improvement insights in practical ways and is delivered to engender feelings of growth, not criticism. When someone is above the line, appeal to their intrinsic motivation. It is only when someone is below the line that a directive conversation is needed.'

Chris agreed. 'Sonya, this stuff is great. I have found your insights on motivation very helpful. I had a situation last week with one of my team members struggling with motivation, and I can see how I would do things differently using the model. One thing I am still struggling with is Liam and the kitchen floor. How would you use this model practically in *that* scenario?'

'Chris, start above the line and appeal to his intrinsic motivation. Clearly, Liam is *not* intrinsically motivated to have a clean kitchen floor. His tolerance for dirt probably far exceeds yours, and I am guessing it is Liam's mother who cares the most. I am also guessing that Liam *is* intrinsically motivated to keep his mother happy. Stop using coercive and extrinsic reward methods such as the pocket money bribe, and appeal to his sense of household responsibility. Get his buy-in and commitment to make his mother happy, and when he cleans the floor, compliment and thank him for his efforts. Show gratitude and admiration, and maybe throw in some extra pocket money as an unexpected bonus.

'If that doesn't work, only then follow the compliance model, but you'll need to step up the ante. Either increase the money to make the bribe worth it or go into punishment mode and withdraw his computer privileges.'

'Okay thanks, I will try that,' Chris said.

'The same approach applies at work. The first prize for your team is that they *want* to work and focus on things they are already motivated to do. You mentioned Fred is more motivated out of work than in it. From earlier conversations we had, maybe Fred feels his positive contributions are interpreted as negativity. His intrinsic motivation to keep the company safe, based on his extensive experience, is not recognised, and so he focuses his discretionary effort elsewhere. Make him feel wanted, valued, and appreciated, and I bet his fire will come back. If that fails, then go for compliance. After all, you are paying a salary, and there is a contractual commitment to earn it.

'Talking about money, linking money to performance may not be a good idea.'

'What?' Chris said. 'Show me the money any day. If you doubled my salary, trust me, you would get superman. I think this crazy idea that money does not motivate was invented by the Human Resources department who want to save on salary bills.'

'Chris, I have never met anyone without money who would disagree with you. Interestingly, the research, as well as my personal experience of talking to friends who have money, suggests otherwise.'

Sonya paged through Chris's *Leader's Guide* and then pointed with her finger to a section and waited while Chris read the paragraph.

MONEY AS A MOTIVATOR

Money is an extrinsic motivator, but it is also a currency of significance. Dan Ariely, the author of *Payoff* (2008), points out, "Money can get you to get people to show up at work. Some of it can actually get people to really care. But, when you think about the knowledge economy, when you think about people's hearts and minds, you think about dedication and so on, it turns out that money can not only not provide you that, it can in fact backfire."

'Sonya, I am not convinced about the limitations of using money as a motivator. I guarantee you if I could promise all my staff a 20% increase their performance would improve.'

'Chris, you are right. There is no doubt that money has a short-term impact, particularly for someone who is lower down the layers of Maslow's hierarchy that we discussed earlier. The money itself may not be a motivator, but the change in lifestyle and reduction in financial pressures are alluring.

'Money is an extrinsic motivator with short-term benefits, but often drives the wrong long-term behaviours.

'Pay people enough money, so they do not feel exploited. Pay them enough, so they do not believe the only way to get an increase is to leave the business. Then focus on other performance enhancement techniques to retain and develop staff.'

'Yeah, well, I lost a lot of money in the Enron scandal back in 2001, so I have a strong commitment to driving the right long-term behaviours.'

With that, Chris waved Sonya goodbye.

RETAINING AND
DEVELOPING THE TEAM

Chris was having an awkward meeting with Emily.

'I do love it here, Chris, and I don't want you to take it personally. It's just that the other company has offered me 10% more money.'

'Well, what if I could match their salary?'

'I don't know. I will also have a shorter commute, and they really seemed excited about me joining their team and promised me lots of training and support.'

'But we have training here, too. Let me see what I can do salary wise, and I am sure I can arrange for you to have some flexibility on your work hours to avoid the traffic.'

Emily looked unconvinced when they parted company.

When Chris met up with Sonya, he briefed her on the situation with Emily. 'I don't understand.' Chris said. 'She said nothing when I promised her a 5% raise in her review, and she never even asked about flexibility.'

'Is flexibility something which is promoted in your business?'

'Well, no, but I am sure under these circumstances I could make her an exception.'

'Chris, key staff retention has to be a long-term strategy. It looks like Emily is emotionally committed to going. Offering her all sorts of benefits to stop her may work in the short term, as it is stressful for her to make the change, but you may only be delaying the inevitable. Possibly if you address what she really wants, you could reverse the situation, but it will probably cost you a lot more now than had you addressed it proactively.'

'Well, we have a new team member starting next month, so I may be doubling up on new recruits now. I will be very sorry if we lose Emily.'

'Talking about new staff,' Sonya said, 'starting well is imperative for new staff members. The first few days on a job have a lasting emotional impact on a candidate. Arrange a formal induction program to help them learn the business and integrate as quickly as possible. Let them get engaged and busy in the first few hours on the job.

'First impressions are important. It is very soul destroying for a new hire to be left alone with no real responsibilities or tasks and told to "read the manual" or shadow another employee by looking over their shoulder.

'Make sure you are ready for them. Have their desk and PC ready and help them integrate socially. Facilitate them meeting key people in the business and clear your diary so you can fast track the induction process.

'Spell out any unwritten rules and etiquette in the company. Explain the disciplines and ground rules you have in place. For example, is it acceptable to work on your laptop during a meeting? Is it permissible to be late to a meeting if a customer delayed you? Can you leave the building without signing out?

'A blind spot that many managers have with new people is forgetting they know absolutely nothing about their current environment. They need direction and training in company-specific aspects to get started, no matter how senior or experienced they were in previous companies.'

Sonya paged through to another section in Chris's *Leader's Guide* that she wanted him to read.

INDUCTION PLAN

A good induction programme could include:

- Compliance and governance onboarding guidance related to HR, IT, finance, and systems
- A strategic overview of the business, including vision, mission, and strategic initiatives
- An operational overview of how the business creates its products and services, sells and supports them and processes the orders (lead to cash process)
- Guidance on the cultural fit aspects with the possible inclusion of a company mentor
- Advice on the people network relationships they will need to foster
- Specific job-related priorities and KPIs, including a peer-level job buddy

Sonya continued. 'Good people are motivated by contributing. But they also want to know that *you* know they are contributing.'

'Agreed,' Chris said.

'Sonya, the prospect of losing Emily has made me worried about Madison. She is a real star. She just gets on with things, and I have very little to do with her as she is very competent and always motivated.'

'Chris, have you heard of Price's law? 50% of the work is done by the square root of the number of workers. You must look after your stars. To retain and motivate a star, make them feel special. Stars thrive on recognition. Just *telling* them they are stars, and sincerely meaning it, is often enough. Managers worry that singling out stars for special treatment may demotivate the rest of the staff. Where the person has only impressed his bosses and no one else, this is very true, but matching recognition for contribution is motivational for everyone, including genuine stars.

'Providing meaningful and sometimes customised rewards and recognition will help to keep them. Give Madison extra responsibility. My guess is that she thrives on a challenge and is interested in the bigger picture. The biggest threat of ignoring stars is that they become complacent. Challenge them to keep raising their own high standards.

'Stars can also make the team lose, though. Some stars can be prima donnas. In May 2015, Margaret Heffernan gave a TED talk where she spoke about the super chicken. Chickens were selected based on the number and size of eggs they laid and then bred with other high performing chickens. Instead of evolving into an elite group, they eventually pecked each other to death. It turned out their performance was based on eating the food of their fellow chickens. As with a team sport, team members should never feel they are above the team or its disciplines. Make sure that they know a star is only a star if the team wins.

'Chris, do you have any poor performers? Nothing will demotivate your team more than you turning a blind eye to an underperforming team member. If someone has a negative and destructive attitude, they need to go, no matter how good their task performance is. If you put a drop of iodine in a glass of water, the water turns purple. Toxic employees have the same effect - they infect everyone.'

'Well, Fred is not a poor performer, but there are parts of his job that are below par. For example, his paperwork is always late, and he refuses to use the systems because he says, "computers are not my thing". It has occurred to me that maybe the team's younger members resent having to fill in for him.'

'Everyone has weaknesses', Sonya said, 'but when a team members' performance falls below the acceptable *minimum* level expected, deal with it early.'

'But that's hard. For example, Rodrigues is relatively new. I have noticed some bad habits of his from his previous company, but I don't want to jump on his case for the first mishap. Won't that demotivate him?'

'Chris, I agree you do not want to be looking for faults and be unreasonable. I am talking about voicing your concerns early. Maybe the first time, you note it and hold your tongue. The second time you need to take action. You could tell him it is too early to judge whether the issue is serious but let him know you noticed. Keep a written record too. This will avoid serious communication problems later. Often, by the time the manager has concluded without doubt that there is a serious problem, it becomes difficult to address as they have silently tolerated the situation for so long and have no record of what has transpired over the preceding months.

'If you find someone is not performing, determine the root cause of the problem. Ask yourself:

- Why is the person not performing?
- Are they the wrong person?
- Are they the right person, but in the wrong job?
- Are they the right person, but they need help?
- Do they need improvement in attitude, or do they lack skills?
- Do they need to learn to apply their skills?

'And of course, if you must dismiss someone, do it within your HR policy. Be empathetic about their feelings. Unless it is a toxic employee, the issue is about their performance in the job, not their worth as a person. If this is done fairly, the person will actually benefit in the long run, so it's a win-win scenario.'

Chris looked worried. 'Sonya, I struggle with critical conversations. Look how badly I handled the situation with Rodrigues. When I write an email, I can review what I want to say before I send it. In verbal conversations, I have to respond in the moment, and I am not good at it. I can't imagine how I will tell someone truthfully about their performance, let alone fire them, without ruining the relationship.'

'Communication is an area we haven't addressed.' Sonya said. 'Maybe we can do that in future sessions.'

'Thanks, Sonya. We certainly have covered a lot in this session.'

Chris thanked Sonya and went back to his office, reflecting on what he had learnt about motivation.

That Friday, after a family night at the movies, Chris said goodnight to Evelyn and his two boys, Liam and Nathan. Chris walked into the kitchen to pour a glass of wine for himself and Gwen. As he picked up the bottle, a mirror image of his 2012 Pinot Noir distracted him. The reflection was coming off the gleaming kitchen floor.

PUTTING IT ALL TOGETHER

Chris met Sonya at the coffee shop. Sonya spoke first.

'This is the last of our planned sessions together. I will leave it with you to discuss with your management if you want to continue with the coaching. Remember, this is not the end of the road; it is the beginning. I have given you some tools to work with and suggestions on how to use them. The rest is up to you.

'One other thing. Remember to look after your own wellbeing. On a plane, you are told to put the oxygen mask on yourself first, in an emergency, and then help others. Management is the same.

'I still remember when I had a sick child at home in my first job, and I mentioned it to my boss, hoping he would cut me some slack. He replied, "Sonya, when you walk through those doors, you are at work. I want you to leave your personal life at the door, and you can collect it again when you go home. I understand that you have a family, but that was your choice, not mine. When you are at work, I need you to be here one hundred percent."

'Today, companies are much more tolerant and understanding of home pressures, but the challenge of balancing personal, family and work needs is harder than ever in this 24/7 always-connected work culture. I think that when people talk about work-life balance, it leads them down the wrong path. At least 50% of your waking hours are spent at work, so if work is not *part* of your life, you miss out on half your life.

'For smart people, most *work* is thinking work and thinking is not linked to your physical location. You think about home at work, and you think about work at home. After a long day at work, if you went home and your partner said, "tell me about your day but do not talk about work," there would not be much to say.

'The challenge is to be aware of when you are thinking *home thoughts* and when you are thinking *work thoughts* and to be *fully there*. Yes, a parent may be worried about their sick child, but they must switch mentally to the client's needs while they present to a client. If the parent can't do that, they should have taken a day's leave because mentally, they are not at work. Half an hour before the presentation, they may have called home to check on their child's wellbeing, and that does not mean they are stealing time from work because when they are at home, they may think about work after attending to their sick child.

'Work happens in our heads, not in the location where we are. The balance gets upset when we are physically in one place with too much time mentally in the other place.'

'Thanks, Sonya, that helps. I often feel guilty about talking about home at work or work at home. This mindset allows me to achieve a balance in my life.'

Sonya wrapped up their conversation. 'If you develop a leadership mindset and focus on people as *whole* people and apply all the operational frameworks we have learnt about, you are well on the way to building a high-performance team.

'Good luck applying all we have discussed. I am enjoying being part of your leadership journey. I always find I learn something new when I am working with smart people.'

Sonya reached into her bag. She produced a file with a list of templates and checklists.

'The secret to management is there is no secret,' Sonya said as she handed the file to Chris. 'But there are some insights and frameworks that will help you. Leading people is complex, with no right answers. Learning to be a good *leader* while also maintaining the necessary disciplines required to *manage* the team is a lifelong journey.

'Just like any difficult or complex task, the starting point is to learn the basics and establish good habits. A simplified, formulaic approach using templates and checklists helps to develop basic rules and disciplines. While these will need to be modified or even replaced when the situation becomes more advanced, having a solid baseline can be helpful. Use these and modify them to make them relevant to your situation. Remember also, in order to break the rules; you first need to master them.'

'Thanks, Sonya, I have learnt a lot. When we first met, I thought that after three months, I would be trained and ready. Now I realise that while I am equipped with the right tools, it will take me a lifetime to master everything. I definitely want your ongoing support. I appreciate the templates and checklists. We have covered so much I hardly know where to start.'

'Chris, I suggest you pick one or two key areas that are a priority in your current situation. Then use the appropriate framework or checklist summarised in this binder until they become a habit.

'I am enjoying working with you. Besides, I think this coffee shop would go broke if the two of us stopped frequenting it.'

Sonya handed him a piece of paper. 'Add this to your file.'

Chris studied the diagram.

TECHNICAL LEADER EXPERTISE WHEEL

❖ ❖ ❖

Sonya explained the diagram she had given him. 'A good leader has a balance of leadership skills. Each skill is like a spoke around the cog. If these skills are imbalanced, you will be a wobbly wheel. The cog represents your core technical skills, and they can grow fatter but will never replace the leadership spokes that transform your expertise into business results.

'We have covered the first four spokes of the wheel: Leadership mindset, Strategic planning, Operational process and Inspiring people.

'You are well on track to becoming a great technical leader and remember to make it a priority to go home at a reasonable hour to enjoy spending quality time with your family.'

'Yes, and no more multi-tasking.' Chris said. 'Now that I have some frameworks in place, I find I am not jumping from one priority to the next, like someone stopping spinning plates from falling. Instead, when I am working on my current priority, I know it's a strategic choice, which allows me to go home at night and leave work behind me.

'Thanks, Sonya, I have found that both my work life and home life have improved, and the feedback I am getting is that my department is moving-the-needle for the business.'

Chris walked back to the office, deep in thought about the learning journey he had been on. There was nothing extraordinary about the theory that Sonya had introduced him to, yet he was acutely aware of how difficult it was to apply. Chris knew he would not be saying goodbye to Sonya. He was only at the start of a lifelong journey of learning.

Sonya remained at the coffee shop and ordered another cup of coffee to buy time before meeting with Chris's boss to wrap up the assignment.

A group of people sat opposite her at a large table, discussing their boss.

'I love our daily stand-up meetings. It helps us align our priorities, and I feel like we operate as a team now.'

'I agree, but they are taking too long. I wish he would take control when people start waffling.'

'Maybe we should tell him. He certainly has been better at listening lately.'

Another team member joined in. 'He is also better at delegating. I am doing more interesting work, and I feel like he trusts me and values my input. He also seems a lot less stressed now that he is not the last person to leave the office.'

'I had a rocky start with him, but recently he seems to have taken me under his wing and has been very encouraging. He seems genuinely in-terested in what I am doing, and I finally feel appreciated for all my good ideas and hard work.'

An older team member chimed in. 'Join the club. It feels like he finally recognises me for my experience. I am no longer watching the clock to see when I can knock off. I actually enjoy being at work!'

Sonya smiled as she watched them return to work. Clearly, they were talking about Chris. She hoped Chris's boss would be as positive.

'Hi Sonya, thanks for meeting me.'

'It's a pleasure,' Sonya replied. 'I hope you are satisfied with Chris's progress.'

'Yes, I am thrilled. I am hearing good reports about his balance between people and process. He seems to find time now for more strategic activities and does not appear to be the workaholic he was before you came along. I think you achieved exactly what we were hoping for. The next challenge is how you can work your magic for him to manage me better.'

'Leading up and across is a whole new topic.' Sonya said. 'You have my number. Call me when you are ready!'

A NOTE FROM THE AUTHOR

I have been leading and managing technical teams for over 30 years and have run countless leadership courses in many countries around the world. I have found that whether you are in Africa, Europe, Australasia or Northern America, the issues are similar.

Sonya and Chris are fictional characters, but I have used them to re-tell true stories and conversations I have encountered in my line-manager roles, business coaching, leadership experiences and many hours being a fly-on-the-wall at airport cafes or local coffee shops. My hope is that you can learn lessons from the experiences of other people.

Learning is a lifelong process, and the day we think we know it all, is the day we have stopped growing as a leader.

Being a good leader requires deep thinking because it is very complex. Being a good manager demands a deep understanding of how businesses really work in the real world, and the frameworks and processes that create order out of the chaos.

I do not for a minute think that I have mastered this subject. I struggle daily with being a more effective leader and manager. My hope is that in sharing my life's experiences, it may help others on their journeys.

Get in touch with me if you agree. I'd love to hear your story. tmanning@tmcglobal.com.au

SONYA'S HANDOUTS

APPENDIX 1 - LEADERSHIP 101 CHECKLIST

	✓
To get buy-in always start with *why* before *what*	
Formally establish the team with clear and unique roles and responsibilities	
Define handover points (the interface customer) as well as the end customer deliverables	
Define *customer measures* before functional *activity measures*	
Balance short-term and long-term activities through *milestone plans*, chunked down into daily *must-do* outputs	
Follow the leadership cycle: *Plan* the milestones and measures without doing, and then *do* without re-planning	
Re-humanise the workplace and treat others as *they* wish to be treated	
Manage and direct the team to achieve basic compliance to high standards and then inspire them to greatness above the compliance line	

APPENDIX 2 - MY LEADERSHIP BOUNDARIES

Use the table below to clarify your key outputs in three categories:

- The things that are part of your core role
- The things that are outside your core role, where you can influence the outcome to add the most discretionary difference
- The things that you would like to change but that are outside your control, and that you should just accept

Core Role	
Can Influence	
Accept	

APPENDIX 3 - MANAGEMENT STYLE CHECKLIST

Use the table below to assist you in deciding whether your primary style should be directive or supportive for different situations.

	Directive Style	Supportive Style
New team	✓	
High performing team		✓
Under-performing team	✓	
Basic team disciplines	✓	
Innovation ideas		✓

APPENDIX 4 - PHASES OF TEAM DEVELOPMENT

Phase 1 (Establishment)

- Directive style
- Define roles
- Create structure
- Define reporting and communication required
- Clarify the difference between activities and outputs (deliverables)
- Identify the customer and customer measures
- Build team relationships
- Focus on 'the why'

Phase 2 (Alignment)

- Make it safe for the team to challenge the setup
- Ask the team what is working and what is not
- Encourage team participation
- Allow and encourage constructive conflict

Phase 3 (Commitment)

- 'We before me' - team affiliation comes first
- Move to a supportive role to optimise performance
- Distribute leadership functions
- Raise the bar

Phase 4 (Autonomy)

- Fully empower the team
- Stay connected

APPENDIX 5 - SETTING UP A TEAM CHECKLIST

	✓
Have I communicated to the team why we exist, so the goals are clear?	
Are these goals aligned across the business?	
Have I specified the *core, extended,* and *external* team?	
Have I arranged a kick-off meeting to get buy-in and align team goals	
Does each person in the team, including me, have job descriptions with no overlapping roles or gaps?	
Is the reporting structure clear?	
Do I have a reporting template and governance structure in place for internal and customer reporting?	
Have I set up regular team meetings so the team can get to know each other?	
Is everyone aware of their team outputs as well as commitments outside of the team structure?	
Does everybody on the team know their unique roles?	
Are we aware of exactly what we deliver as an output?	
Do we know specifically who we deliver that to?	
Have we asked our customers how they define and measure success?	
Are both lead and lag measures and targets agreed and reviewed and tracked weekly by the team?	
Does everyone on the team have documented and aligned KPI's?	

APPENDIX 6 - FOCUS AREA TEMPLATE

Summarise your team's outputs into three to five focus areas. For at least ONE of these areas, work out what the strategic objective is and define a mini project - an initiative - that will improve the customer-defined measurement of success. Define the milestones (usually monthly) and next major action for each initiative.

Focus Area 1:

Strategic Objective	
Initiative	
Milestone (measure)	
Next Action	

APPENDIX 7 - TEAM DISCIPLINES

	✓
Have I shared the minimum behavioural standards and attitudes expected with my team?	
Are the team fully aware of their limits of empowerment including spending limits and decision-making?	
Are the HR policies clearly understood and enforced?	
Have I defined the limits of flexibility regarding time-keeping and whereabouts?	
Are deadlines for reporting and administration clearly understood and enforced?	
Have I established a set of well-understood ground rules for the team, on things like meeting disciplines, emails, reports and proactive communication?	

APPENDIX 8 - MEASURES AND REPORTING

- ◆ Measure *trends* to assess longer term root causes
- ◆ Measures must be repeatable and reliable
- ◆ Measures should be objective and relevant
- ◆ Only measure what matters - ask myself '*what will I do with these measures?*'
- ◆ Don't have too many
- ◆ Develop a simple dashboard

	✓
Have we agreed how we will review performance and what communication methods we will use?	
Are you continually tracking and reporting on the results of the plans against measurable outputs and targets?	
Has a regular review process been set up to review monthly and quarterly measures	
Do all team members do a weekly and monthly report where measures are tracked and plans and actions converge?	

WEEKLY REPORT FORMAT

Use this template for your weekly written report

- ◆ Key metrics (actual vs target)

Completed last week	
Planned this week	
Top issues or concerns	

APPENDIX 9 - MEETINGS PPPP

PPPP: Planning, Purpose, Process, Payoff

Planning: To *plan* the meeting for success, ask:

- Is a meeting the best method available?
- What will this meeting cost versus the benefits gained?
- How much time is really needed? Make it as short as necessary.
- What stakeholders need to attend?
- What role do I want each person attending to play?

Purpose: Define the reason for the meeting:

- Ask yourself what the primary purpose is: Is it making decisions, sharing information, solving problems, planning, celebrating success?
- Write down the purpose of the meeting in a single sentence

Process: Describe the format to be followed:

- Ask, *'What is going to happen and how is this going to be organised?'*
- Use an agenda that includes a timed outline of issues covered and lists each attendee's names
- Attach any pre-meeting reference data, previous minutes, actions, reports or homework, for consideration

Payoff: Describe the benefits for the people attending:

- Clarify the benefit of all participants dedicating their time to attending the meeting

APPENDIX 10 - DAILY HABITS AND COMMITMENTS

One of the key steps to mastery is to practise your core skills until they become a habit. It is important to establish a daily habit to plan your day, finish your most important things first and remind yourself of your daily self-improvement commitments.

- Triage everything that *could* be done
- Decide what *must* actually be done
- Decide what to delegate
- Prioritise the "*most urgent, most important*" items (i.e. do first!)
- Block time off in your calendar for legitimate urgent interventions and unscheduled work
- Chunk the task to fit the timeslot and then make sure it is 100% finished

Triage List	✓

Jot down any important reminders to add to your calendar.

Reminders	✓

My One Thing:

Choose ONE thing that you will commit to completing by the end of the day, ideally linked to a strategic initiative. Once it is done, mark it as complete. ✓

'If I do nothing else before I go to bed tonight, I will complete:'

Date	My one thing	✓

Daily commitments

Remind yourself at the start of each day of your daily commitments and confirm that you did them at the end of each day

Date	My commitments:	✓
	- Plan my day - Do first things first - Connect with people - Prioritise those people and things that are MOST important to me - Make a positive difference in every-thing I do	

APPENDIX 11 - PERFORMANCE MANAGEMENT

Lead above the line and manage below the line

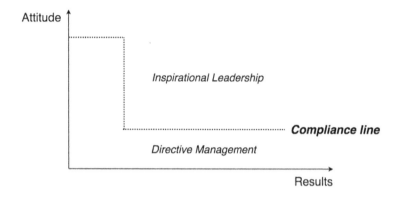

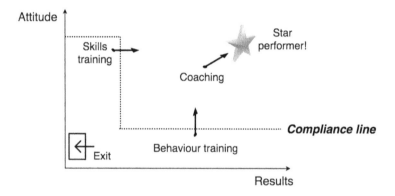

APPENDIX 12 - FACE-TO-FACE TEAM REVIEW (MONTHLY)

- ◆ Do you know where the company is going? (Discuss big picture, strategic outlook)
- ◆ Where are you going? (Discuss career and development aspects)
- ◆ What is going well? (Discuss strengths and successes)
- ◆ If you were your own coach, what would you improve? (Discuss any lessons learnt)
- ◆ How can I help you? (Discuss any support needed and get feedback on the management style that will get the best out of them)

APPENDIX 13 - TECHNICAL LEADER EXPERTISE WHEEL

GLOSSARY

CSF - Critical Success Factors

KPI's - Key Performance Indicators

Gen Y - Also called millennials (born between early 80's and mid to late 90's)

NPS - Net Promoter Score

OKR - Objectives and Key Results

SDT - Self determination theory defines our primary psychological needs as autonomy, relatedness, and competence.

SMART(S) - Specific, Measurable, Achievable and Agreed, Realistic and Relevant, Timebound, Stretching

SWOT analysis - Strengths, Weaknesses, Opportunities, Threats

RECOMMENDED READING

Berger, J., *Unlocking Leadership Mindtraps: How to thrive in complexity,* Stanford University Press, 2019.

Cane, S., *Quiet - The power of Introverts in a World that Can't Stop Talking,* Penguin, 2013.

Glen, P., *Leading Geeks: How to manage and lead people who deliver technology,* Jossey-Bass, 2003.

Grant, A., *Think Again: The Power of Knowing What You Don't Know,* Viking Books, 2021.

Kotter, J., *Accelerate,* Harvard Business Review Press, 2014.

Lencioni, P., *The Five Dysfunctions Of A Team*, Jossey-Bass, 2002.

McChrystal, S., *Team Of Teams*, Random House, 2015.

Morgan, J., *The Future Leader,* John Wiley and Sons, 2020.

Pink, D., *Drive: The Surprising Truth About What Motivates Us,* Canongate Books, 2009.

Schmidt, E., *How Google works,* John Murray, 2017.

REFERENCES

Allen, D., *Getting things done*, Piatkus publishing, 2007.

Ariely, D., *Predictably Irrational*, HarperCollins, 2008.

Blanchard, K., *The One Minute Manager Builds High Performance Teams*, HarperCollins, 2004.

Bregman, P., *Eighteen Minutes: Find your focus*, Orion Books, 2011.

Chabris, C. & Simons, D., *The Invisible Gorilla*, HarperCollins, 2010.

Collins, J., *Good To Great*, Random House, 2001.

Covey, S. R., 2002. *First things first*, Simon and Schuster, 2002.

Drucker, P., *The Effective Executive*, Collins Business press, 2006.

Fowler, S., *Why motivating people doesn't work*, Berrett Koehler Publishers, 2014.

Goldsmith, M., *What Got You Here, Won't Get You There*, Profile Books, 2012.

Kahneman, D., *Thinking, Fast And Slow*, Farrar, Straus and Giroux, 2011.

Kaplan, R., & Norton, D., *The Balanced Scorecard*, Harvard Business School Press, 1996.

Koch, R., *The 80/20 manager*, Hachette Digital, 2013.

Kroeger, O., *Type talk at work*, Tilden Press, 1993.

Lipnack, J. & Stamps, J., *Virtual Teams*, John Wiley & Sons, Ltd, 2000.

Lissaman, P. B. S., & C. A. Shollenberger, *Formation Flight of Birds*, *Science*.

Maslow, A., 2012. *A Theory Of Human Motivation*, Start Publishing. Retrieved from https://www.amazon.com.au/Theory-Human-Motivation-H-Maslow-ebook Original manuscript published in 1943.

Marquet, D., *Turn the Ship Around!: A True Story of Turning Followers into Leaders,* Penguin, 2013.

McGregor, D., *The Human Side Of Enterprise*, McGraw-Hill Professional, 1960.

Rath, T., *Strengthsfinder 2.0*, Simon and Schuster, 2007.

Sinek, S., *Start with Why,* Penguin, 2011.

Taylor, F., *The Principles of Scientific Management,* A public Domain book, 1911. Retrieved from https://www.amazon.com.au/Principles-Scientific-Management-Frederick-Winslow-ebook

Tuckman, B., *Developmental sequence in small groups*, Psychological Bulletin, 1965

Zhuo, J., *The Making of a Manager*, Penguin, 2019.

ABOUT THE AUTHOR

Trevor Manning specialises in real-world training and the development of technical people who have transitioned into management. His mission is to help Smart People transition to Inspiring Leaders.

During a 30-year career in the IT and telecommunications sectors, Trevor worked his way up from specialist design engineer to board level. This journey from expert to middle manager, and then on to the C-suite, has provided Trevor with the breadth and depth of knowledge in how companies really operate. His experience in establishing and developing technical teams from a group of technical experts to a high-performing team forms the basis of the insights shared in this book.

He has diverse experience having run global operations and has worked in South Africa, UK-Europe, America, and Australia in a range of companies from a giant electric utility to a small start-up software company. This has given him insights to help people in a variety of real-world situations.

Trevor has experience managing and leading people in mature, stable environments with fixed structures and processes, and the chaotic start-up phase of a fast-growing new business. These environments exposed him to the challenges of recruiting and developing teams to meet the companies' growth plans in addition to downsizing during lean years.

Trevor runs training programs worldwide, including at Oxford University (UK) and the University of Wisconsin-Madison (USA), as part of their Continuing Education programs for engineers.

In addition, Trevor has written a down-to-earth, practical, how-to series of books on leadership, targeting technical people, called the "Help!" series.

Contact the author at:

Email: tmanning@tmcglobal.com.au

www.tmcglobal.com.au

OTHER BOOKS BY TREVOR MANNING

Microwave Radio Transmission Design Guide
- *Publisher: Artech House, 1999.*

Help! What's the secret to leading engineers, 2017
- *Order from Amazon*

Help! I need to master critical conversations, 2018
- *Order from Amazon*

MICROWAVE RADIO Handy Reference Guide, 2019
- *Order from Amazon*

Milton Keynes UK
Ingram Content Group UK Ltd.
UKHW042044291024
450359UK00004B/66